T0069750

To Keera With Love

Abortion, Adoption or Keeping the Baby: The Story of One Teen's Choices

Kayla M. Becker
with Connie K. Heckert

Sheed & Ward

Dedication

To my daughter, Keera, with love. And to other young women like myself who are forced to make the most difficult decision of a lifetime.

This project is supported, in part, by a Faculty Development Research Grant from St. Ambrose University, Davenport, Iowa.

Copyright© 1987
Connie K. Heckert
Third printing, 1993

Child of My Heart© 1987 Sidney Jeanne Seward. Written for Kayla Becker and used by permission.

All rights reserved. No part of this book may be reproduced or transmitted in any form or by any means, electronic or mechanical, including photo-copying, recording or by an information storage and retrieval system without permission in writing from the Publisher.

Sheed & Ward™ is a service of The National Catholic Reporter Publishing Company.

Library of Congress Catalog Card Number: 87-62400

ISBN: 1-55612-072-9

Published by: Sheed & Ward
               115 E. Armour Blvd. P.O. Box 419492
               Kansas City, MO 64141

To order, call: (800) 333-7373

Contents

Preface

There's an old cliche about time healing all wounds. This may be true. Time, however, never wipes away precious memories or diminishes the importance of people who mean a lot to us. My love for my daughter, Keera, the baby I had out-of-wedlock at age eighteen, will never lessen.

Today, there is a strong trend for young women—once it has been decided not to choose abortion—to keep their babies instead of allowing them to be adopted. For some, this may be the best answer. But there are many options open to pregnant teens today. They have more control over the adoption process and are able to make decisions affecting the future of an infant daughter or son. I wanted my baby to have two parents. I wanted them to raise my daughter in the Catholic faith and I didn't want them to smoke cigarettes. I wanted a mother who could stay home with my baby until she was of school age. The couple I chose fulfilled my criteria.

These are several reasons for writing this book. I think young women have choices open to them if they are informed and aware of the options. I want to share my story with other teenaged women, with parents, and with professionals who counsel these women. Perhaps the experiences I have had and the options I discovered that were available to me will be helpful to all pregnant teenagers. Hopefully, the information presented in the appendices will be useful in decision-making processes. A final reason for undertaking this book project, and perhaps the most important to me personally, is that someday my daughter—and other adopted children—may know this story, and realize these decisions aren't easy or without pain to a birthmother, her family, and friends.

There were many people who shared in this difficult experience. Here, I would like to thank my family—Corey and Aaron Becker, Ray Phillips and Michael Becker—and most of all my mother, Kathryn Bohn, for being so terrific and supportive throughout my pregnancy. She was more than a mother—she was a friend. I'd also like to thank my good friends Eileen, Margaret (Madge), Heather, Amy and Jamie. They didn't stop seeing me when I became pregnant and were always around to share my tears and my heartbreak. They were with me when I needed someone to talk to and are the best kind of friends anyone could ever ask for.

Most of the people in this story are represented by their own names. Exceptions are those whose identity we feel, for various reasons, should be protected. We have created pseudonyms for the adoptive mother and father, Kayla's obstetrician and adoptive lawyer, the social worker, and Keera's biological father and his parents. The names of teens identified in the appendices have been changed to comply with T.A.P.P. (Teenage Pregnancy and Parenting Program) policy. Although Keera's birth name has been changed by the adoptive family, she is known throughout the story as Keera.

K.B.

My co-author, Connie Heckert, and I would like to thank others who supported this project and helped make it possible: Robert Heyer, Editor-in-Chief, Sheed and Ward; Father Michael T. Mannion, author and Catholic Campus Minister and Director of the Newman Center at Glassboro State College in New Jersey.

Also, Denise Cocciolone, Exec. Dir., Birthright, Inc.; Vicky Thorn, Coordinator Project Rachel and Co-Dir. of the Office of Respect Life, Archdiocese of Milwaukee, WI; Mary Ann Hughes, Exec. Dir., National Youth for Pro-life Coalition; Wanda Franz, Ph.D., Vice President, National Right to Life Committee; Ernest L. Ohlhoff, Exec. Dir., National Committee for a Human Life Amendment; and William Pierce, Exec. Dir., and Mary Beth Seader, Dir. for Pregnancy Counseling and Maternity Services with the National Committee for Adoption. J. Michael Byers, Pearson Foundation, Inc.; Ellen Walsh, Exec. Dir. and Patricia A. Cramer, R.N., M.S., Regional Rep. for Alternatives to Abortion International were also helpful.

Additional interviews were conducted with Linda Cloghessy, Childbirth Educator, Childbirth Education Assoc. of the Mississippi Valley, Inc.; Helen Brown, Counselor, Teenage Pregnancy and Parenting Program; John Aitken, Attorney at Law; and Tom Fedje, Exec. Dir., Maternal Health Center. Also, thanks to Carol Livermore and Connie Langer for "being there."

We are humbly grateful to the adoptive parents who so generously allowed us to publish photographs of the baby.

Finally, we would especially like to offer our gratitude to members of the faculty and administration of St. Ambrose University in Davenport, Iowa, for providing a Faculty Development Research Grant which partially supported this project: Donald J. Moeller, Provost; Dr. Margaret Legg, Bonnie Lindemann, and Dr. Patricia Kennedy. And finally, to our professional readers, all of whom are published authors in their own right: Willetta Balla, Judie Gulley, Delores A. Kuenning, Janice Oliver, Sidney Jeanne Seward, and Christine Walkowicz.

K.M.B./C.K.H..

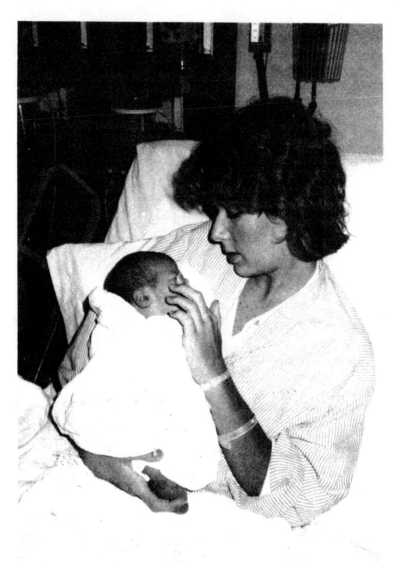

Keera at birth

Prologue
The Day of Indecision

My stomach was upset. I wiped my palms on my baggy maternity slacks and walked out of my bedroom. I knew signing the papers to give my baby up for adoption would be hard. I told myself I could do it. But now, after I had held and fed my daughter, Keera, I didn't want to.

I'd had nine months to make up my mind. Now my eyes are dry, but I'm crying inside. Keera is my baby. No one will ever be as close to her as I am right now. I've carried her inside me for so long. I've felt her happy kicks . . . sometimes so strong they hurt my ribs.

Why should I give her up? She is mine!

I've made my decision. The lawyer is coming this morning. In those traumatic first days after the pregnancy was confirmed, I hadn't known what to do. I turned to Stephen, the baby's father, for advice and support.

I was heartbroken when he told me that, in his opinion, an abortion was the only answer. I loved him so much. Now, he had let me down. I was frightened. What would happen to me? All my friends were going off to college in the fall. I'd be having a baby—a baby whose father had rejected both of us.

In those long months before the baby was born, I made up my mind I must do my best to deliver a healthy child. Once I stopped vomiting and could keep food down again, I tried to eat lots of fruits and vegetables— even spinach that I detested. I stopped drinking anything with artificial sweeteners because I had heard that wouldn't be good for the baby. I took long walks at the shopping mall and avoided sweets. And always there was that frantic question: What should I do?

This morning at nine o'clock—Saturday, August 31—my attorney is coming here with the papers.

I knew I had to sign them.

Mom and I were in the kitchen. She crossed from the cupboard to the sink in the process of making coffee. She was dressed for work in a terrific black suit. Only two months ago, two years after resigning her position as co-anchor at a local news station, she had opened a designer clothing store in an exclusive colonial shopping and business complex in Davenport, Iowa.

I reached into the refrigerator for milk and poured a glass, hoping it would help calm my nervous stomach. I took it back to my room, glancing into the living room as I went.

Ray Phillips, my stepfather, sat on one of the over-stuffed white sofas, reading the morning newspaper while he watched the circular drive below for the lawyer's car. The past year had been a hard one for him too. He had experienced the failure of his first electrical contracting business in the economically suffering Quad-Cities market. How many people had the area's major employers—John Deere, Caterpillar,

J.I. Case and International Harvester—laid off work? How many hundreds of homes were for sale as residents looked for jobs elsewhere? I didn't know, but I knew our area was worse off than most.

How could I keep adding to my mother and stepfather's problems? They had so many things to think about. Yet they had stood by me through all of this. No matter how busy Mom and Ray were, they found time for my brothers Corey and Aaron, and me when we needed them. They certainly didn't need to have me further complicate their lives and add to their financial problems with an unplanned, out-of-wedlock pregnancy.

When the doorbell rang, it was like a bell tolling the final hour. Mom let the visitors in and called to me in my bedroom. I slowly got up from the bed and went to answer the door, avoiding Ray's concerned gaze as I passed him in the living room.

My lawyer, Robert Nash (pseudonym), said hello and stepped back from the blue door to let two women enter the foyer. I showed them into the living room where Mom and Ray were standing. Mr. Nash introduced his wife and the other woman, Lois Nelson (pseudonym). Both women had come to serve as witnesses as was required by the law in our state. Lois Nelson was a friend of the adoptive couple.

"Your home is beautiful," Mrs. Nash said, looking at the plants around the room. "Someone around here certainly has a green thumb."

Mom said thank-you and mentioned the advantage of having large windows. She started to have us all sit in the living room. Abruptly, she changed her mind, suggesting that the dining room table might be better for signing papers.

If I can sign them, I thought.

Ray sat at one end of the formal table, John Nash at the other nearest the living room. I took the chair next to him and across from Mrs. Nash. Mom sat by me and across from the other woman. The table seated ten; chairs remained empty between Ray and Mom.

The lawyer cleared his throat and began explaining the papers I had to sign today.

"Kayla, after you sign this, you still have 96 hours to change your mind. The baby will be placed in Lois's home because she is a friend of the adoptive couple," he said.[1]

He explained that I had to testify in front of these witnesses and began to ask me questions.

"Have I ever coerced you in any way into giving this baby up for adoption, offering you money, or something that could constitute bribery?"

"No," I said, looking up from my hands at Mr. Nash.

"Have I made any statements to induce you to sign these papers?"

"No."

"Have I promised you anything in exchange for your signature?"

1. Laws on severing parental rights differ from state to state. In Iowa, a birth mother cannot sign a custody release for 72 hours after she has delivered to insure she is free from effects of any drugs. Then she has 96 hours to unconditionally change her mind. After the 96-hour period has expired, she may change her mind, but she must stipulate on what grounds the release of custody should be revoked: i.e., fraud, coercion, misrepresentation. A court hearing held one to two weeks later is for entering an order terminating the biological rights between the parents and the child. The final step takes place after a period of approximately six months, when the adoptive parents may petition the court to finalize the adoption.

"No."

"Kayla, I know this isn't going to be easy. But by signing this adoption paper, you still have 96 hours to reconsider your decision," he explained again. "After the 96 hours, it will be your burden to allege and prove to a court why your parental rights should not be terminated. Do you understand this?"

When I said I understood everything, he handed me the papers. I stared at them as Ray's voice broke the silence.

"Now, if Kayla has 96 hours, does that mean she has until five o'clock Wednesday morning to let you know if she changes her mind?" he asked.

The attorney nodded his head. "Yes, that's correct."

"If anything should happen to the baby, I'd be informed, wouldn't I?" I asked. "And what happens if the parents are killed in a plane crash or something like that? Could I ever get the baby back?"

Bob Nash shook his head. "No," he said. "Once you sever your rights, you have no more responsibility for this child. It's the parents' decision as to who her legal guardians will be."

There was an uncomfortable silence before he went on.

"The adoptive parents are good people, Kayla," he said slowly. "They're both under thirty, they're Catholic and they don't smoke . . . everything you specified for an adoptive couple. These things have been assured."

I swallowed but the knot that swelled in my throat remained. I couldn't control the tears that filled my eyes.

"Kayla, you've handled all of this so well. The pregnancy . . . the delivery . . . ," Mr. Nash said, searching for words, trying to keep the process moving toward the final conclusion. "I know this has to be hard for you."

"Would you like some coffee?" Mom asked. She jumped up from the table without waiting for an answer, her black heels clicking like rifle shots across the hardwood floor to the Spanish ceramic tile in the kitchen. She came back with the china service on a tray. She set it down, filled the cups and passed them out, one at a time from her side of the table.

"Do you take cream or sugar?" she asked, in a controlled voice. After everyone had been served, she sat back down.

The lawyer took a sip of the steaming, hot liquid, then said, "After you sign this paper, we'll go to the hospital and the baby will go to the home of the friends of the adoptive parents."

"No," I said. "I don't want her to be switched around from home to home. I want her to go right to the adoptive parents. I want her to start getting the love she needs right away."

I looked away. After Mom had divorced my father, we had moved thirteen times in twelve years, sometimes following her career, other times because a landlord had sold a house after we had fixed it up.

Mom's voice brought me back to the present.

"Oh, Kayla, are you sure you want to do that, Honey?" Mom asked. I could tell she was surprised. "You have three days to make up your mind. That's why the law is written this way."

"No, I've made up my mind about this."

"Oh, okay," said Mr. Nash. "Then she'll go right to the adoptive parents' home. But you'd better be sure that this is what you want to do, Kayla. Because if you change your mind, it's going to be pretty hard for them to give her back after they've had her."

"No, I've made up my mind. I'm not going to change it."

I tried to read the legal papers. The quiet room was like a hot and humid summer day in Iowa even though the air conditioning was on full blast. Finally, I picked up the pen the lawyer had laid on the table. I could hardly hold it, my hand was shaking so. A picture of Keera in her tiny pink blanket flashed through my mind. I remembered her dark eyes looking up at me, searching at the sound of my voice. I could feel the strength of her sucking mouth on my little finger.

The line where I was to sign disappeared in a blur. I put the pen down and picked up a tissue from my lap, wiped my eyes and blew my nose hard.

I could hear Mom crying. There was a rustle of cellophane as Ray pulled a pack of tissues from an inside pocket of his three-piece vested suit. I looked up to see both women on the other side of the table crying. *I'm sure they're both mothers*, I thought. *They both have children. They couldn't do this.* I looked at the lawyer. Even his eyes were filled with tears.

Everyone was waiting for me to sign this piece of paper. But no one could say, "Sign it, Kayla. Get it over with." At the same time, no one could say, "Don't sign it, Kayla. You want to keep Keera? Then keep her. She's yours, you don't have to give her up."

Mom cleared her throat. "Kayla, if you're not ready to do this, we don't have to do it. It can be put off until another time."

"Well, Kathryn, we have to do something today," the lawyer interrupted, contradicting Mom. "The doctor discharged the baby and she has to leave the hospital. If you don't sign today, then you'll have to make provisions for the baby to come here. You're not giving me permission to take this baby and place her."

"Kayla! Honey, if you bring her home, you'll never let her go," Mom said.

I sat there, staring at the pen, crying. All week long, Hurricane Elena had been raging off the East Coast. It was nothing compared to the turmoil within me. I still wore the white slacks and pink, green and blue striped maternity blouse that had become a uniform for me before the birth of the baby. But now, I felt empty.

All around the table, I could hear the others sniffling, sharing my pain.

"Kayla, if you can't sign it . . . ," Mom's voice drifted off.

"No, I can sign it. I can sign it. I have to do it. I'm not going to change my mind. It's for the best. She needs to be in a better home than I can give her."

I wiped my eyes and again picked up the pen. I tried to sign the paper, but my hand was shaking so hard, I couldn't do it. A fresh wave of tears flooded my vision.

"Kayla, I just don't know if you can go through this," Mom said.

Poor Mom, I thought. *This is hard for her too. It's her first grandchild. She said Keera looks just like me when I was a baby. She blamed herself when she found out I was pregnant. But it wouldn't have mattered. I would have done it anyway. I loved Stephen so much . . . .*

"Kayla, why don't you wait a day or so? You're so upset right now."

"No, I'm going to go through with it. It's for the best. I have to do it."

I took a deep breath, as I wiped my eyes and nose with a fresh tissue. Concentrating on the pen and paper, I pushed all thoughts of Keera from my mind. I braced myself, scribbled my name, *Kayla Marie Becker*, and released the pen. It clattered to the table. I dropped my head to my arms, as the lawyer took the paper. I lay there, sobbing . . . for myself and for Keera, but also for Mom and Ray—and Stephen who had wanted nothing to do with her.

I barely heard the people around me get up. Faintly, I heard one of the women say, "I'm sorry we had to put you through this." When the house was still, Mom walked back into the dining room and put her hand on my shoulder. I looked up at her reddened eyes. The words that came from my mouth sounded familiar, yet alien to me. My tongue was controlled by my heart.

"Oh, I wish I wouldn't have done it. I wish I wouldn't have done it."

"Kayla, I wish you had let them take her to Mrs. Nelson's home to give you a few more days to think about this decision."

I sat up and looked at my mother, sobbing. "I didn't want to do it! I didn't want to do it! I wish I wouldn't have done it!"

"Then you have only one choice, Kayla. You have to call the lawyer and tell him you changed your mind and the baby is to go to Mrs. Nelson's to give you a few more days."

"I can't. You do it," I said, placing both hands flat on the table.

"Kayla, you have to do it."

"I can't, Mom. I just can't."

"Oh, all right. I'll call the hospital and see if I can catch Mr. Nash." She went to the wall phone in the kitchen. I listened as she dialed and talked to the nurse on duty. I could visualize the nurses' station on the third floor maternity ward at St. Luke's Hospital. I could tell by Mom's side of the conversation that my lawyer hadn't arrived.

If he takes the baby to the adoptive parents' home, it will be too late!

Mom left a message, asking Mr. Nash to call immediately. "It's very important," I heard her say.

The minutes slowly ticked by as we waited anxiously. When the phone rang, Mom, still hovering nearby, grabbed it.

"It's just what I was afraid of," I heard her say. "Kayla changed her mind. The baby should go to the friends' home to give Kayla more time to think about this."

Mom listened, then said, "Just a minute. Kayla, you've got to talk to him. You're the mother and this is your decision."

I got on the phone, visualizing the attorney's frustration as I started to talk.

"I want her to go to the friends' home. I need a little more time."

"Is this your decision?" he asked me. "You, and only you, are the one making this decision?"

"Yes," I said. "Oh yes, it's just me."

As I hung up the telephone, I sighed deeply. I felt as if a terrible burden had been lifted from my shoulders. If I had been a prisoner on death row, and the President of the United States had granted me a three-day reprieve, I couldn't have felt more relieved. I had just been given a gift of 96 more hours to decide whether I would keep Keera or give her to two strangers . . . two strangers who wanted her just as badly as I did.

But at this moment, I had absolutely no idea of what I would do: give up my baby forever, or keep her. I only knew that I wanted terribly to make the best possible decision for all of us.

At Social worker's home

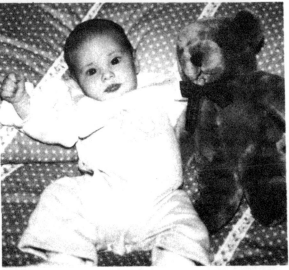

Keera at six weeks

1

Fenelon

I stared at my younger brother, Corey. He was lying on his back, pounding his fists and heels on the floor. His flushed cheeks contrasted sharply with his light blond hair and fair skin. His plaid shirt was twisted, straining the buttons.

"Why isn't he coming?" he screamed. "Dad said he was taking us to the park tonight. Where is he? Why isn't he coming?"

Mom frowned slightly and tried to calmly answer him.

"Corey, stop that. Your Dad must have gotten busy—maybe he'll call later on and explain."

"You're always making excuses. He didn't call last night, either." Corey rolled to his side and kicked the refrigerator.

I hated it when Corey got so upset. I was disappointed Dad wasn't coming, but I didn't throw a fit like Corey. No one threw a fit like Corey.

"Your father works hard all day. He needs time to relax, Corey," Mom said as he rolled onto his back. She grabbed his ankles and held them fast to the floor. "Listen to me, Honey. You just saw your father last Saturday. It's not like he never comes to see us. When people work hard they need a rest . . . a vacation. Your father works hard with people who have lots of problems. He needs a rest from people. It doesn't mean he doesn't love you. He does. I do. So please stop this." Her gaze held Corey fast.

Corey sniffled, but he didn't resist Mom's gentle, but firm touch. When he nodded, she let go and helped him up. He pressed his face into her body as she wrapped her arms around him. A few moments later, when his sobs had quieted, he pushed away, and as Mom watched, he walked over to me and we went into the living room.

It might sound funny to some people, but the first years of my life were spent in a group home. Fenelon Group Home is located on Fenelon Place in Dubuque, Iowa, high atop a bluff. From where we lived, we could see the entire city with its snow-capped houses and businesses in winter, and the exciting Mississippi River with its rising, swiftly flowing waters in spring.

By the time we had moved to Fenelon, we had already lived in five different locations! I was born at University Hospitals in Iowa City on my Grandma Bohn's birthday—November 1, 1966—amidst great celebration by relatives and friends. Family was important to me as a child. It's still a strong part of my adult life.

Two weeks after my birth, I made my first visit to church at St. Wenceslaus Catholic Church in Iowa City where I screamed my head off all the way through the service. Religion, too, played an important role in our lives when I was a young girl. My first birthday was celebrated by eating cake and attending Mass on All Saint's Day. I was so proud when, as a small child, I learned my first prayer . . . with the help of the host of television's syndicated program, *Romper Room*:

God is Great,
God is Good.
And we thank Him for our food.

Before I was born, my father earned his undergraduate degree in social work at Loras College. When he worked on his master's degree at the University of Iowa, we lived in an apartment. We moved first to Des Moines for eleven months and next to Coralville for four months before relocating on Pear Street in Dubuque. It was March of 1968. Twenty-one months later, we moved to Fenelon. That's the place I remember best, probably because it was my first *real* home.

Even at the age of three, my life seemed to center around family and motherhood. My baby book, a gift from Aunt Glenda, contains this hand-written entry by my mother:

My first song was "Three Little Kittens." I loved books and always liked Mommy to read before bed. I loved to play records at two years of age and dance with the music. I knew all the songs and was such a good dancer. I also played Mommy "lots" and my favorite baby was Terri. I always slept with her and took good care of her.

Mom went by her childhood name of Kathy, then. She and my father, Mike Becker, were both employed in social work. For three years we lived in the third floor apartment—servants' quarters of the historic 13-room home. The second floor was reserved for the girls who lived with us. The first-floor dining room—where we shared our meals—was huge. We have pictures of birthday parties where that long table was filled with my family and friends, waiting for cake and ice cream, wearing pointed hats with blue, black, red and yellow dots.

Fenelon was a halfway house for young girls who couldn't live at home for one reason or another. Most of them were 15 or 17, but occasionally one would be older, 20 or 21. Either they couldn't get along with their parents, they had drug problems, or they had been in trouble with the law. It was my parents' job to reinforce the parenting process being conducted by the natural parents or the state-employed social workers—if the girl was a ward of the state. Each girl had to sign a contract and abide by the rules. Mom and Dad tell me they made several trips to the hospital during those years with any one of a number of the girls who had overdosed on drugs. A couple of the girls became pregnant out of wedlock while we lived there.

After Corey came along, my father, Mike, seemed to give Corey more attention than me. He had always wanted a son and he'd never had a brother. As Corey grew older, Dad and Corey shared an interest in sports that sometimes left me out, even if unintentionally. Today, Corey is probably the closest to our father.

To tell you what my early life was like, I have to go back to old photo albums and silent home movies Mom and Dad took of us. My parents bought the camera and projector after Corey was born. Corey had even lighter blond hair—much lighter than my brown hair—that glistened like cornsilks in the sunlight. My hair was straight and long and it fell three or four inches below my shoulders. Sometimes I wore it parted in the middle (my bangs always split naturally in the center) or Mom made twin pony tails on the sides with rubberbands and yellow, pink or blue ribbons.

I still have the doll I treasured when I was two. She was my *first* baby, the only doll that I ever really liked. Her hair is painted on and she squeaks. Her eyes are pale blue and she has tiny creases under her eyes, a perfect nose and lips and little ears that you can stick your finger into. Today, she wears a zippered, pale yellow sleeper and underneath her pink dotted Swiss dress is pinned a green checkered diaper trimmed with lace. I remember splashing in the bath with her, then taking her head off and pouring the water out. Once a leg came off and I cried until Grandma Becker sewed it back on.

Although Corey and Dad shared their favorite sports activities, Dad continued to play with me. One fall I remember Dad and I worked together, raking leaves. We only had one rake so I used a broom. Once we had amassed a huge pile, Dad grabbed me, laughing, and pulled me down into the crackling leaves. Our father loved to play with all of us on the bed, at the park, and in the living room in front of the fireplace with its old, white mantel and the shelves lined with books.

Christmas was a special family time for us. I was so excited about ripping off bows and tearing into wrapping paper. Mom and Dad sat back and watched, smiling at us. Dad was wearing a beard then and sat cross-legged with me on his lap and put one arm around me, tickling my cheek with his whiskers. I can remember his strong and gentle strength and that he always had a kiss for me when I greeted him at the door or said good-by as he left for work.

During the day, Corey and I used to play together—even after Aaron was born—because we were close in age. We'd bury each other under stuffed toys—Teddy, Bunny, Raggedy Ann and Andy and Monkey—in a brown swivel chair in the living room. Then we'd push the chair around and around while we sang. I must have been a dull baby—the only trouble Mom says I ever got into was when I pulled pans out of the cupboards.

I never even wanted to run away from home. There were too many good times . . . when we used to play *Ring Around the Rosey*, Corey, Mom and I. Later, after Aaron was born, we three danced together. I can't remember a time when I wasn't dancing. I had my own special step—back and forth. When Mom told me to put a variety into my movements, I'd just speed up. Maybe I wasn't a great dancer, but I loved wearing my pink leotard, ballet slippers and white socks for practice.

Often, Mom and Dad would pack nine of us into the station wagon for an afternoon at Murphy Park. The girls—Beth, Donna, Bonnie, Chris and Cathy—from Fenelon would play softball while we played on the swingset until Mom and Dad joined them. I guess we were the only family some of them felt close to so they liked to clown around. One day while we stood by laughing, they made a pyramid on their hands and knees, climbing on each other's backs with *Dad* on top.

I remember Maureen and Becky best of all. Maureen had long dark hair and took me window shopping at the plaza. Becky was a redhead with a blonde strip in the front. Later when we moved back to Fenelon Place, Becky lived across the street with her little girl. There were other times when Mom and Dad took all of us out for hamburgers at the end of the day. The girls used to call our Mom "Mom" just for fun. Often, one of the waitresses would ask Mom if we were *all* her children. It made us laugh.

Jenny was another one of the girls from those early years at Fenelon. I remember her wearing a blue blouse and jeans, calling to Corey and me, and inviting us into the recreation room.

"Come on, Kayla. We're going to do *The Monster Mash*. That's it. Keep on bopping." She would laugh at us—they would all laugh at us—trying to keep up with them, bobbing to the quick tempo. Mom says they worked out a lot of frustrations dancing with each other in that room.

One day, Dad came home from work but he was quiet and sad. He didn't kiss me or hug me and he ignored Corey and Aaron. That night, my parents had a long, quiet talk in the bedroom. They never raised their voices or argued in front of us. Not long after that, Dad moved to an apartment of his own.

It wasn't until years later that we learned that he was depressed and suffering from burnout. He spent all his waking hours with so many people who had problems. Mom had suggested that Dad could move to an apartment until we could join him. But then, he had met Jane—the first of four wives—and wanted to marry her. My parents had been married for seven years.

One afternoon, when I was five, I went to play by myself on the seesaw in back of Fenelon. The seesaw was broken. I looked at it with frustration, thinking Corey had probably done it, and went back into the house.

"Mom, the seesaw is broken," I told her. "Could you have Daddy fix it?" Our father had built a sandbox for us and was handy at making minor repairs. I knew if it could be fixed, he would do it.

Mom looked away with tears in her eyes. Then she pulled me closer and put her hands on my bare arms.

"Kayla, we're going on an adventure," she said, bending her knees and crouching so she could talk to me face to face. "We're going to move to a new house where it will be just our family."

"Is Daddy coming too?"

"No," she said, her tears spilling over. "But it will be fun. We'll explore a different house and a new neighborhood. We'll work together fixing it up."

I nodded, trusting my mother. She had never let me down before.

Daddy never did come back to live with us. Soon after that conversation, we packed Monkey, Raggedy Ann and Andy into boxes for moving. I said a sad good-by to the broken swingset and Fenelon House where we'd had so many good times as a family. The girls even cried to see us go. The swingset never did get fixed—at least that I know of.

Grandma Becker and I wanted my parents to get back together. Sometimes I'd pray for that to happen. Each time my father divorced and re-married, I'd find myself hoping Mom and Dad would reconcile. After the third divorce, I think I finally realized there was no hope of being a family again.

For three years, Mom and Dad parented more than 100 adolescent girls in Dubuque. Now Mom needed a job to support us and applied for one with the Department of Social Services. During the next three and a half years, she interviewed prospective food stamp recipients. Some days she'd come home and her mood was sad and quiet. I think that's when she put the huge letter, "M" up on her bedroom door. The "M" stood for meditation as in Transcendental Meditation. The first time she explained it to us, we didn't really understand. But once, just once, I knocked on the door when she had her "M" up, and I was spanked for it.

We learned to leave her alone. Mom said that it was the TM that helped her get through so many of those hard days.

After the divorce, we lived in rented houses in safe neighborhoods close enough to walk to school. Mom made sure of this because she worked and couldn't take us. But to insure that the neighborhood met her standards, she had to pay a big share of our income for housing. When Dad had his own financial problems and didn't send support payments, which happened occasionally, finances stressed Mom. There was more than once that all we had to eat was a peanut butter sandwich and a glass of Kool-Aid . . .with promises of cookies and milk on payday.

After the divorce, we used to shop for groceries on Sunday nights. When there weren't support payments, we qualified for free food stamps and Mom said she needed the help. But at the same time, she was so embarrassed to use them that she picked a slow time to shop so she wouldn't run into any of *her* food stamp clients. She hated it so much that she finally stopped using them.

After the divorce, there were only four of us continuing on a series of great adventures that were to take us from one address to another and from Dubuque to Davenport, Iowa. Even then I knew it was hard being the child of a single parent. We all loved each other and we were happy together, but there were many things we couldn't have because there was only enough money for essential food, clothing, and housing. It would be many years before I knew the real meaning of the word, luxury.

That first move in 1972 was only the beginning.

2

From House Mom
to Media Anchor

My mother once told a local newspaper reporter that in the early 1970s she was the kind of woman readers would see described in a magazine like *Better Homes and Gardens*. By 1982, she felt she belonged more in a periodical like *Working Woman*. As a single parent who had gone to work and to school full time while trying to raise three children by herself, her philosophy of life changed markedly.

My mother probably has affected me more than any other person. Whenever I had a problem, I always went first to her. She protected us, consoled us and always took care of things. My mother didn't give up easily, and she still doesn't.

The day before we were to move from Fenelon, the house Mom had rented caught on fire. If Mom was flustered, it didn't show. At the last minute, she found a temporary location for us until the charred house was repaired.

That first night in a strange house was scary. It's still vivid because I remember we didn't have any furniture. Corey, Aaron, Mom and I slept on the floor together, snuggled close for security. Here, there was no "Monster Mash" or lots of girls chattering noisily at dinner.

After Dad moved out, he called and came to visit when he could, but it wasn't the same. One time, Mom said, six months had passed before he called or wrote. Sometimes I missed him. Other times I was angry that he wasn't there. Much later, I understood that my parents didn't live together because they didn't love each other. But I never thought that meant they didn't love me, or Corey and Aaron. We never blamed ourselves for their divorce. Mom wouldn't let us.

When I started kindergarten and my classmates asked me what my father did for a living, I quietly responded, "My parents are divorced." It made me feel different to be from a broken home. As I grew older, I talked with classmates whose parents were divorced. Most of them said they missed the absent parent.

Now, as I look back on my childhood, the only thing I would have changed would be all the moving we did. It didn't make me feel insecure because my mother knew that her attitude would generate feelings, so she always talked positively about relocating and made it seem like an adventure. I just didn't like the bother.

There were several times when we decorated the house and the landlord sold it, so we had to move again. The house on Visilea was like that. It was a three-bedroom ranch. Mom wallpapered the kitchen, put up shutters and painted the bedrooms at her own expense. Of course, we were lots of help!

At that time, Donna, a girlfriend of Mom's, lived with us. She had left her husband after 27 years of marriage and needed a place to stay. She moved in for a "day or so" and stayed six months, fixing up the basement into her own little apartment. One time Dad came to visit and got real mad at Mom for some reason. He pushed the back basement door and broke the lock. Donna was the handy one—she built her own walls and fixed the broken lock for us. She helped take care of us when Mom had to be gone.

The first Christmas after my parents were divorced, we had a real tree, Mom's handmade ornaments and there was lots of company. Mom always made sure the house was filled with friends—especially around the holidays. She didn't want us to feel lonely or to be sad about Dad not being there. I still have my biggest gift from that Christmas: a sleeping bag.

When Mom started dating, at first I didn't know she was going out with another man. Maybe that's because we popped popcorn and all went to a drive-in.

Not too long after the divorce, Mom started dating Dick Tracy. (He gets kidded about his name a lot.) He was a substitute for our father—if there was one—because he played with us and took my brothers fishing. Mom dated him off and on for about eight years. She broke up with him after he came back from working on the Alaskan pipeline. But that's a whole new story.

I remember I liked David Corona in particular. He was an art director for a publishing company who designed the cover for a psychology book, and put a picture of Corey and me inside. In 1986, when Mom opened her new business, he designed her stationery and advertising logo. I liked him because he talked to us more than some of the men Mom dated. He took us to Chicago once where his mother, "Granny," lived and baked cookies. She must have liked us because I remember getting homemade cookies in the mail after our visit.

Mom made one stipulation for her male friends. If they liked her, they had to like us, too. She wasn't like one woman she knew who hid her small children in the basement when her dates came to the front door. More than once during those early years, I watched Dick change Aaron's messy pants. But it was David who was there to handle one important crisis.

Mom had had a bad day at work. She came home tired and cranky and put Corey and Aaron into the big, old-fashioned bathtub with bubblebath so they could soak. One of my brilliant brothers grabbed the bottle of bubblebath and added more to the flowing water . . . until the bathroom was filled with bubbles!

Mom walked in with me right behind her and said, "That's it! I'm leaving. Good-by!" She turned and left, walking past me downstairs and out the door to the picnic table directly below the bathroom window. Later we found out she sat there, listening.

I started to cry, believing every word. "See what you did?" I yelled at my brothers. "Dad left; Mom can, too."

Corey, standing in the tub with bubbles sticking to his body, and Aaron, sitting there, joined my chorus. "Mom left," Aaron howled. "She's gone!"

David came in and squatted at the tub's edge, trying desperately to console all three of us at once. He pulled the plug to allow the water to drain and some of the bubbles to wash away. "No, no, she's not gone. Your mother wouldn't leave you."

But we knew in our hearts that it was possible.

Mom tells about one month when single parenthood was particularly bleak. She learned that the landlord was selling our home out from under us, she was losing her job, and her child support payments had stopped. As if that weren't enough, she had been home all week with strep throat. Although I was too young to know it, I was watching what it was like to be a single mother. And it was hard.

From 1973-1974, Mom served as technical advisor to low income elderly. She used to come home telling funny stories about work. Once she talked about a fat social worker who hid candy bars in her desk and snuck bites when she thought no one was looking. Even then my mother was health conscious.

One day Mom came home from work, exhausted, and a neighbor lady and I met her in the yard.

"I don't know who's babysitting your children, but whoever it is, she's not doing a very good job," the neighbor said.

"Oh no," Mom said. "Now what?"

"Corey and Aaron were playing on the roof today. If they had fallen off, they could have been killed."

Mom's frown told me that Corey and Aaron were in for it. And I knew she'd tell the babysitter about it, too. But it was typical of the crises all parents have with young children. Mom was always getting called home because one of us needed stitches. When Aaron received a new bicycle for his birthday, he immediately rode into the back of a parked car. One day Corey dropped a brick on his head. In all, Corey has scars for three sets of stitches on his forehead. These problems aren't unique for a parent. But a single parent deals with each problem alone.

Later Mom found a new job, and rallying support from her social service supervisors, she started back to school. Clarke College, originally a Catholic School for women, later became co-ed and expanded its curriculum. Mom decided to major in communications. She took Corey, Aaron and me there once to hear African music in a listening booth for one of her assignments.

Mom borrowed money to pay for classes. For a while, she was working full time, going to school full time, and raising three kids alone.
She'd work all day, come home and feed us dinner, promising she'd
have more time for us during the summer. At night, she attended classes. After school, she'd sleep for a while, setting the alarm for two
o'clock so she could get up to study. She'd go back to sleep and get up
in time for work. We lived with that pattern for the next two years.

But even with my mother's crazy schedule, she made it a point to put
us first. We always knew that she wanted our lives to be better. There
were lots of weekends when she didn't date, but spent all of her time
with us. She always made us feel important. She encouraged us in
schoolwork and play.

The house on Rush Street was an old, two-story home. Here, we
wallpapered Corey and Aaron's room, but the landlord paid for the
materials this time. Mom's bedroom didn't have any heat and in the
winter it gets cold in Dubuque, Iowa. But what I remember most about
that house is that we had a garden in the back yard where we worked
together, sharing our laughter and showing each other our blisters. The
results of our hard work was worth a few days of sore hands. In the
summer, Corey, Aaron and I would go out to the garden and pick carrots, wash them and eat them under the shade of a nearby oak tree.

Mom framed the self-portrait I drew when I was in first grade. I had
long brown hair, big eyes, a button nose and a wide smile. Even then I
must have imagined myself a dancer—my feet in this picture were
pointed out. I colored my top green and I drew a heart-shaped neck-
lace for my throat. I must have liked colors—I used lots of crayons to
draw horizontal stripes. Mom says my drawings were always happy pictures.

The media classes at Clarke led to internships at KDTH Radio and
into television at KDUB where Mom stayed for a year. When she started working in the media, she decided to use her full name, Kathryn,

with her surname, Bohn. By then, I was taking ballet lessons two or three times each week. Afterwards, I'd go up to the station—it was located on the tenth floor of the Dubuque Building—and wait for Mom.

More than once, we called Mom at work. She said it was *always* when she was up against a deadline.

"When will you be home for dinner?" Corey would ask.

"Soon, Corey," she'd reply. "I shouldn't be late."

Or, I'd call when Corey and Aaron were fighting.

"Mom, Corey and Aaron are at it again," I said.

She sighed. "Put Corey on."

First she talked to Corey, then she asked to talk to Aaron. Finally, I'd have to get back on the line.

"Kayla, you have to take charge when I'm not there. You're the oldest and you need to help me."

"But Mom, they won't listen....."

"We can talk more about this when I get home. I have to go now."

In 1978, Sylvester Stallone was in town for the filming of the movie, *FIST*, in Dubuque. One day, Mom took us to watch. There were crowds of people lined up along the barricades. After watching for what seemed like forever, we saw Sylvester Stallone walk by only a few feet away.

Mom paid for a tight, curly perm so she could work as an "extra" in the movie and told us how much trouble the local reporters were having getting close enough to talk to Sylvester Stallone. No one from the station could get an interview. But leave it to my mother to get an exclusive that resulted in a two-hour taped special, as well as a chance to host a corresponding one-hour live special!

I never felt like I had a question or a problem that Mom wasn't there to help, although it's possible there were moments when she wasn't. Most of the time, I remember being with my friends. Whenever Mom had to be out of town, Corey and Aaron went to our friends' house, the McDonald's, who later went with us on vacation to a cabin on Virginia Beach. I often stayed with Mom's friend, Vayla, where we baked cookies and bread together.

Switching schools so much was another thing I didn't like much about my childhood, I suppose. Before I had graduated from high school, I'd been in eight different schools—four in Dubuque and four in Davenport. I sometimes wonder if an "Army brat" lives the same kind of life—frequently moving, starting over in new schools and learning to make new friends. This lifestyle later affected my decisions about Keera's well-being. I wanted a more normal upbringing for her. I didn't want her to feel the way I had that first day in every new school: frightened and shy.

It wasn't until I was in the fourth grade at Lincoln School that I met my first boyfriend. His name was Steve. He held my hand, but he never gave me a kiss. I liked him for about a year. That was the year Mrs. Scott was my teacher. Of all the teachers in all the schools, I think I liked her the best. We put on plays and she and I got along well.

Fourth grade was a memorable year for other reasons, too. I flew to visit my father in Milwaukee. To make connections, I had to fly to O'Hare Airport in Chicago. This childhood experience left a lasting effect, let me tell you!

Not long after my parents were divorced, my father married Jane, an employee with the mentally retarded at Catholic Charities, and moved to Galena. My brothers and I visited them and enjoyed it. They lived in a nice house with two Irish setters. Mom told us Jane didn't like us, because she wanted to have children and they couldn't. That marriage lasted a couple of years before Dad went off on his own to Milwaukee. There he met and married Wendy, who worked in a hotel.

Sometimes Corey, Aaron and I visited Dad together. Other times, we'd go individually. This particular time, I was alone. Mom had told me there would be someone waiting to help me. But when I got off the plane, there were people everywhere but no one looked eager to help me! I was scared. I wasn't used to taking care of myself. I went up to one person and showed him my ticket.

"Do you know where I'm supposed to go to get on this plane?" I asked.

"Go ask that gentleman." He pointed to a man in a business suit.

"Do you know where I'm supposed to go to get on this plane?" I asked again.

"Go ask that woman at the counter," the man said. Always trusting, I followed the advice.

"Do you know where I'm supposed to go to get on this plane?"

"No. Go down to that counter and ask the man standing there."

By now, I was in tears. I knew I didn't have much time before my next plane was supposed to take off.

At the counter, I would have asked again, but the man behind it was too busy checking tickets and assigning seats for his passengers. So I asked a woman standing in line.

"*No me explico por qué !Qué va!*" She pointed to a man further down the hall.

I kept telling myself not to worry. You won't get lost, don't worry, I said over and over.

The next man gave me a map of the airport and pointed me in one direction. I trusted him and went a little way and asked another man. He told me to get on a bus. Still trusting, I climbed the steps and was told how much money to put in the coin receptacle.

"I don't have any money," I said, looking at him with bewilderment.

"Then get off," the impatient driver retorted without looking up. "You're not going to take the bus."

By then I was bawling my head off. I wasn't even supposed to get on a bus! I was supposed to take a plane. I went back inside the airport and one man helped me. I had to walk about a block—out of the building—to where I was supposed to board my plane. I finally got there, but I nearly missed take-off. As I buckled my seatbelt, I let out a sigh of relief and dried the tears on my sticky face. I couldn't wait to see my father.

He was there, standing alone, when I walked into the airport. I told him my story and he laughed. Later, when I told Mom, she laughed too, making light of the experience, saying everything was okay now. Fine. I still won't go to O'Hare Airport without a traveling companion. To me, it's a scary, terrible place—especially for a young child traveling alone.

In 1977, Mom learned of an opening for a feature reporter and morning anchor at WOC (Channel 6) in Davenport, an NBC affiliate. She applied and was hired, but later she told us she was nervous about starting a new job in a new city. Most of all, she was afraid of the challenge of moving three children from one town to another by herself.

Money was the main reason Mom said she considered different employment. It would pay $225 a week. She was only making $180 at the time for 60-hour weeks with no overtime compensation. The added income would have helped buy so many things we needed. She went to her station manager and told him about the offer; he agreed to meet WOC's terms if she would stay.

Overnight, she made her decision to remain in Dubuque. When she went in to talk to the station manager, however, he reneged on his agreement and told her his top salary for her would be $220 per week. Mom couldn't believe he would let her go for only $5 a week! It became a test of wills. He stubbornly watched her pack her things and leave. He had the last word after all. He withheld her vacation pay. She never did get it.

I was in fifth grade when Mom prepared us for our biggest "adventure" yet. We moved again, this time to Davenport, Iowa.

3

Career Moves and Family Relocations

"Kayla, there she is! There's your Mom! Kathryn Bohn!" From where she sat Indian style, Juli pointed to the television screen.

"I know that's my Mom," I said. "Don't you think I know what my mother looks like?"

We moved in June to Davenport, Iowa. Our new home was in an apartment complex. This place had an indoor swimming pool, and I liked that just fine. So did Corey and Aaron. Wednesdays were "Kids Nights" and we went almost every week. We had a lot of fun playing. I always wore huge goggles because the water got in my nose and I couldn't open my eyes underwater without them. A few times, Mom took us to the pool and watched while we played; usually, we went with our friends.

By now, I was twelve years old and a sixth grader at McKinley School. It had been six years since my parents divorced. We were used to not having my father around. Sometimes we still missed him, but mostly we managed on our own.

I had my own room in our new apartment; Corey and Aaron shared one and had their own bathroom. I was still taking ballet lessons and had lots of ballerina costumes. One dresser drawer was full of dance slippers. I used to take a sheet of plywood out into the hallway on the second floor landing, plug in the radio and practice my dancing there.

Some days, after I jumped off the school bus, I'd run home with my new friends, turn on the television and watch my mother reporting a story. That made me pretty special in my friends' eyes. They thought it was really neat that I had a TV celebrity for a mother. At first I was impressed too; after a while I became blasé about it. When people made a fuss about her job, it made me feel warm inside. To them, I'd just say, "It's no big deal." What I liked best about her jobs in the media was meeting people like newscaster John Barton in Dubuque with his black hair flecked with distinguished gray. And Andrea Zinga, a news anchor, or Thom Cornelis, an award-winning sportscaster, in Illinois and Iowa.

That year in current events class, we talked about Golda Meir, Prime Minister of Israel, who had died, and the Panama Canal treaties which were ratified by the U.S. Senate. Another topic was the Jim Jones massacre. The world was shocked by poisonings initiated by leader Jim Jones at the Peoples Temple in the jungle Guyanese commune. I had to hear about it in school, but none of that affected me. I was more interested in meeting new friends and practicing my ballet.

In my world, Mom was adjusting to a new job and a new city. It wasn't easy. She said her news director, who has since moved from the area, was prejudiced against working women. He tolerated them under his management because of Equal Opportunity laws. He told her she'd never succeed in the media business. He seemed to be proving out his prediction by making her daily life miserable.

I felt awfully sorry for her when he constantly corrected her pronunciation of words until she thought she couldn't pronounce her own name. (Mother's speech was really good.) After every radio broadcast, he called to tell her about all the mistakes. He never complimented her—no matter how hard she worked. She used to say she could never reach his expectations, but now she feels he didn't want her to. He seemed to want subservient women in the newsroom. If he couldn't make them that way, he wanted them out. And he wanted my Mom out. She was "the new kid on the block" and she thought he was especially hard on her.

His attitude made me mad. It made more all the more angry because I couldn't do anything about it.

At home, Mom couldn't eat even after she fixed us a nice meal. Her stomach was tied in knots from stress. We ate our meals in the kitchen at a little table where Corey and Aaron always talked more than I did. But I noticed Mom wasn't eating anything.

"Don't you like the spaghetti, Mom?" I asked.

"My stomach is upset," she said. "But you eat yours. Okay, Honey?"

While we ate, she sat there and talked to us.

For six weeks she continued to eat very little. I thought she was on a diet. But one morning I heard her vomiting, and I got scared. What if something happened to Mom? How would I take care of my two brothers? I wasn't old enough to be a mother.

She was so sick physically and so miserable emotionally, that one day at work, she laid her head down on her desk and cried. Someone told her she should see a doctor. She did and was told she had ulcers. He put her on a soft diet: yogurt, baby foods and cream of rice cereal. I remember watching her eat from the jar and wanting to taste the Gerber chopped pears. Or was it peaches?

When Mom went for a second opinion, that doctor put her into the hospital for three days for tests. I remember one of Mom's girlfriends stayed with us. From the tests, Mom learned she was eating all the wrong things for her problem: spastic colon. This doctor said she should be eating high amounts of roughage, not soft foods! She had to change her diet and she needed to learn how to handle stress . . . or she would meet an early death. That really scared her and me too.

After that experience, Mom seemed to change and take charge of her life. All she could think about was her three children without their mother.

She decided to meet with her news director and tell him how she felt. She was tired of his behavior, and he had no right to treat that way. She took a deep breath, marched into her boss's office, and told him exactly how she felt about his attitude and the way he had been treating her.

We could tell Mom was happier when she came home from work now. That made me feel better too. She told us the news director was more fair in his dealings with her.

I was so glad things seemed to be improved. It was awful watching my mother eat baby food for dinner every night. *Now*, we were into lots of salads and fresh, raw vegetables. We still are, as a matter of fact.

While Mom was at work, Corey, Aaron and I played around the apartments with our friends unless we were in school. We lived next to a golf course and we walked through the woods—along the trail past Creeping Charlie, dandelions, and yellow wildflowers—to the hole in the chain link fence. As I went through the opening, I felt like *Alice in Wonderland*. We entered another world and hunted golf balls. Sometimes we got into trouble; we weren't supposed to be on the golf course. But it was worth the risk. We sold balls for a quarter or fifty cents to Mom or other people in the apartments.

When we weren't hunting golf balls, we played football or baseball on the apartment grounds. I was a pretty good hitter then. The boys wanted me on their team when we played softball. We also explored Duck Creek. We lived in the apartments a year and a half and learned to know the creek and the area pretty well.

There must have been a farm nearby. I remember the rooster crowing. And lots of times there was a lawnmower running. But I didn't pay much attention because there were so many kids my age to play with.

When Juli moved in to the apartment complex with her Dad and brother, Chris, we became good friends. My Mom dated her Dad once, and we became excited, thinking we'd be sisters.

I remember sitting on the steps and talking while we lived at those apartments. We'd drag board games out to the front steps or play "Truth or Dare," a game where you had to choose either truth, or dare, and answer the challenge. If someone said double dare, everyone would have to do the dare. I almost always chose truth.

We were playing hide'n' seek the first time I was kissed. Jim, one of my neighborhood chums, and I were hiding behind the trees next to the fence. All of a sudden I felt a kiss on my cheek.

"Why did you do that?" I asked. I was surprised.

"I don't know," he said, grinning. That was the last time I hid behind *anything* with Jim!

One night after work, Mom almost danced into the apartment and swooped me up in a bear hug.

"Guess what? Consultants visited the station today and guess whose feature story they picked as one of the best?" she said, happily. "Mine! They liked my work and told the news director he should use me more."

I smiled at Mom. It was impossible not to be happy when she got excited.

"What does that mean?" I was doing my homework at the kitchen table and appreciated any excuse to quit.

"That means, Suzy Q," she said, "that I'm going to have more responsibility and I'll be assigned better stories to research."

We saw more and more of our mother on television. I had always thought she looked terrific. But now she had more confidence. For two years, she worked hard to build up her reputation and improve her career. That's one thing about my Mom. She applies herself totally to any task at hand.

While I was still in junior high, we moved to a house on Duggleby Street. There was a mulberry tree in the back yard and we planted tomatoes next to the house. My friend, Juli, moved to the same neighborhood shortly afterwards, and she and I used to walk to school.

Mom had one of her friends sink a pole next to the driveway for a basketball hoop. When the owners asked us to move so they could sell the house, it made us mad because they wouldn't let us take our pole. Once in a while, I drive by the house and still see it.

The tree is still there where we tied Duffer, our Lhasa Apso puppy. He was a small, white dog with hair that flopped over his eyes. When we moved from Duggleby, we stayed at the Blackhawk Hotel and had to take Duffer from the tenth floor apartment to the "one's," or one-way streets, to do "his business."

WQAD-TV, an ABC affiliate based across the Mississippi River in Moline, Illinois, hired Mom in November of 1980. She had an opportunity to produce instead of reporting feature stories. She says the day she told her WOC news director she was leaving, he blew up and told her to get out. He made her leave the same day and she didn't even get to say good-bye to everyone.

The new job required Mom to work behind-the-scenes. Before long, she was promoted to anchor the Weekday Magazine show when the former hostess left for Texas and the opening occurred. Mom helped put that show into top ratings and was later promoted to co-anchor of the 6 P.M. and 10 P.M. news. Her salary almost doubled from $13,000 to $25,000 overnight. She was happy about the big jump in pay, but she still thought she was paid less than her male co-anchor.

Mom met Ray Phillips, a contractor and developer, when she interviewed him for a WQAD-TV news story. Later she sent him congratulatory flowers for the fine job he did renovating the Blackhawk Hotel in downtown Davenport.

At first, she says she was hurt when he didn't call to acknowledge the flowers. Later, she learned it was because he didn't remember who "Kathryn" was! But that didn't stop Mom. She called him and suggested the first date.

When I met Ray Phillips, I thought he was nice, but I didn't like him as well as I liked David Corona, the one who had been giving Corey and Aaron their famous bubblebath. Ray was tall and lean, had thinning hair and wore wire-rimmed glasses. He was very distinguished looking, but I thought Ray was old. At the time, Mom was in her late thirties; Ray was in his sixties. She dated him off and on for about two years.

Ray was good to us and he and Mom were pretty serious. He helped create our dream house. He bought an average home on Marquette Street and used his expertise as a contractor and developer to expand it for us to live in until they married.

I was so excited about it. Every day after school I walked to the house to see how far workers had progressed. In all, two bedrooms, three baths, a recreation room, a greenhouse for Mom and a hot tub off the master bedroom were added. I remember Mom made trips to Chicago with an interior decorator to furnish it. The living room had hardwood floors, a fireplace, and white, overstuffed furniture. There were large tropical plants near almost every window. We moved there when I was a freshman, about 13 or 14 years old.

It was like being transformed from poor to rich when we moved into that house. I had my own bedroom and bathroom and could stay in there forever if I wanted. It was like having my own little apartment. I had everything I needed: my own towels, toiletries and small appliances. It was heavenly not to fight anymore to use the bathroom—or the blowdryer! No one yelled at me because I spent so much time working with my hair or putting on makeup. And Mom bought a wonderful picture of a ballerina to hang on the wall over the bed. I loved being there.

My friends Amy, Jamie, Eileen and Madge came into my life when I started to attend classes at Assumption High School, a Catholic private institution within walking distance from the new house. I met Eileen first. She had a round, healthy face and short, light, brown hair, parted on one side. Eileen told me I could walk to school with her because we were neighbors.

Later, I found out my friends envied me. They said they were jealous because I had a famous mother and lived in such a big, glamorous house. But I told them the same thing I'd always said, "It's no big deal." I really didn't think it was a big deal. I felt I deserved this big change. But I didn't feel like a different person because of it. I still remembered eating peanut butter sandwiches and Kool-Aid because there was no money for anything else.

Jamie looked and acted so much like me that teachers asked if we were sisters. We both wore our hair long with the bangs parted in the middle of the forehead. I was wearing braces by then, but teachers still couldn't tell us apart.

Madge was bubbly and outgoing. She had long, dark hair that fell below her shoulders. She wore it tied back with a barrette.

During my freshman and sophomore years, Amy was another one of my best friends. She wore her hair long too, only it was blonde and parted in the middle.

That first year, Eileen, Madge and I went to a State Basketball Tournament in Des Moines, Iowa, with Eileen's parents. The three of us shared a room next door to theirs. While Eileen and Madge swam, I stayed dry—I couldn't get my new perm wet. After a while it was boring, watching everyone have a water fight. So when Joe, a senior, asked me to go walking, I left.

"How did you do on the math test?" he asked.

"Okay, I guess. Math isn't my favorite subject," I answered.

We strolled along the hotel corridors. "Would you like to go back to my room? I've got some beer there."

"Okay." It wasn't a big deal. Lots of the kids drank beer. After all, Joe was a senior and I trusted him. And I didn't drink much. That night, I took only a sip to be polite.

We sat on the edge of the bed, talking. Joe took my hand and held it. He leaned over and kissed me.

Suddenly, there was a pounding at the door.

"Kayla! Kayla! Are you in there? Open the door!" I recognized Eileen's and Madge's voices.

"It's after ten o'clock. You've missed bedcheck."

We walked to the door and Joe opened it.

"Kayla, we've been looking all over for you," Eileen said. "We've been running up and down the halls in two hotels trying to find you. We walked through one door and a security guard yelled at us, 'Get out of the hotel.' I felt like a criminal."

I was surprised to see the frightened looks on their faces.

Madge's long, wavy, brown hair was still wet from the pool. "Eileen had to tell her parents a lie to cover for you. Why didn't you tell us you were going somewhere?"

"You were too busy with the water fight to notice me. I couldn't get your attention. So after a while, I gave up and left. I wasn't lost," I said defensively. "I was with Joe." If I could survive O'Hare Airport, a Des Moines hotel didn't seem so tough. After all, *this* time I wasn't alone.

Joe and I said good-night and Madge led the way, marching back to our rooms. We hadn't been in bed long, when suddenly, the fire alarms went off. It seemed as if no one would sleep that night. The lights from the city flashed through the open drapes.

Eileen and I looked at each other, rolled our eyes, and covered our heads with pillows. When we looked to the window, there was a student on the ledge outside. He was locked out.

There was a knock on the door. It was Eileen's parents.

"Girls, did you set off the fire alarms?" Eileen's Mom asked.

"No," we protested in unison. We had our suspicions, however.

"Any one of a number of people we know could have done it," Madge volunteered. "But we were right here. We didn't have anything to do with it."

That year seemed like the beginning of my dating experience. From that point on, I felt more grown-up.

During my sophomore year, my braces were removed. I was so excited about going to school the next day to show everyone. I walked up to Jamie and flashed my teeth.

"Jamie, look, I got my braces off." It was then I noticed her eyes were red from crying.

"Jamie, what's wrong?"

"Didn't you hear, Kayla?" she asked. "Amy's mother died suddenly." Her tears flowed again.

No one noticed I didn't wear braces anymore. All day long, everyone I knew who was a friend of Amy's was grief-stricken. When I went home, Mom called the school to let me out of classes the next day. Jamie, Eileen, Madge and I went over to Amy's and stayed with her. I felt so bad. But at the same time, I was glad it wasn't my Mom.

When Mom told us she was going to marry Ray Phillips, I felt happy for her. But I didn't know what it would be like. I guess I was a little afraid. I didn't know if our life would be better after she was re-married. I only knew that it would be different. The next time I visited Dad, he didn't say anything about it. We just didn't talk about it.

The wedding took place on June 11, 1983, when I was 17. It was considered the social event of the summer. I was seventeen. There were stories in the local newspapers and a Sunday morning bridal brunch. The wedding reception for 200 guests was at our house.

Mom announced she would keep her television name, Kathryn Bohn. She chose a 1930s fashion theme and hired a Dixieland Band to play at the reception. The day before the wedding, we had white tables and white wooden chairs set up. In case of rain, Mom rented yellow and white tents with scalloped edges. She solicited advice from her former greenhouse expert at WQAD before planting geraniums and marigolds so the yard would be pretty. Across the railing of the deck stretched a colorful banner with Mom and Ray's initials. They read like call letters for a broadcast station: CELEBRATE! KBRP, June 1983.

Rick Wickline, co-owner of The Hairkutters, a top salon in the Quad-Cities, came to the house to style hair for the women in the bridal party. It was fun, but I was afraid it was a wasted effort. We wore close-fitting, creamy white hats—they looked like enlarged skullcaps with billowy matching scarves at the side. Our dresses were street-length with three tiers and each had a matching scarf draped around the hips in the '30s style. My dress was rose pink; Mom's sister, Beth, wore one in a hot pink color and Mom was in a tiered, ivory dress covered with lace.

Because Mom was a local celebrity and Ray had so many business associates, half the fun was the guest list. The broadcasting media was represented in droves. The mayor of Davenport was there and many prominant citizens attended, including a congressman and a senator. Most of Mom's relatives came to the reception and almost all of Ray's were there.

Hors d'oeuvres were catered from a business in Iowa City, but as a family, we had picked strawberries at the summerhouse and dipped them in chocolate for the wedding, much like we had dyed Easter eggs as children. Our elegant table stretched across the dining room and was filled with cold salmon, fresh fruit, crisp vegetables and delicious cheeses.

Bartenders in black tuxedos busily mixed drinks and poured Asti Spumonte into stemmed glasses. All over the yard and house there were ladies in elegant summer dresses and men wearing suits, interspersed with the wedding party in formal attire. I felt prettier than I ever had before. I tried to imagine what my own wedding would be like someday.

Cars were parked along the main thoroughfare of Marquette for blocks on the side streets. After the reception, Mom and Ray climbed into a loaned, white antique convertible decorated with streamers and "Just Married" signs. Mom and Ray honeymooned for two weeks in San Diego and then drove up the California coast.

The next month, I started dating Stephen.

4

The Father of My Child

I first met Stephen Webster at a party in July 1983, and I didn't pay much attention to him. After that, I didn't see him for a long time. In September 1984, I ran into him again at the library. He said he was working on a research paper about the military service.

I was with Jamie and she seemed to be impressed. "Who was that?" she asked. "He's gorgeous!"

"Just a boy I know," I said.

Stephen was eighteen, I was one year younger. He asked if I'd go out with him. The next night he picked me up at my house, and we rode his motorcycle to the library. This was our first date.

He was about 5'11" tall, not really muscular then and he had big brown eyes and dark, short hair. He had some acne problems that seemed to be healing.

I guess I was attracted to him because he was fun. He liked to party a lot and I knew sometimes he drank too much. But he was careful about how much he drank when I was going out with him. It was fun dating someone who rode a motorcycle everywhere. He was really nice to me, he said he cared about me, and I trusted him. He was easy to talk to, and before long, I liked Stephen a lot. He was the first boy I was ever serious with.

It was a whirlwind romance. That fall I applied for a job and started working at a department store. When I wasn't working, we went to movies: *Reckless* and *Apocalypse Now.* We saw John Travolta and Olivia Newton John in *Grease* . . . and Robert DeNiro in *The Deer Hunter.* Several times we rented videos so we could see them at his house. Stephen especially liked watching one military movie that starred Cheryl Ladd.

I celebrated my 18th birthday on November 1st—not with Stephen, but with Eileen, Jamie and Madge. They took me to a Mexican restaurant where the employees sang, "So it's your birthday . . ." and put a sombrero on my head. I was so embarrassed; I wanted to fall through the floor. We laughed so hard I was in tears and had a stomach ache.

One Friday night, I had to work until closing at the department store so I was going to meet Stephen and my friends at the football game. Eileen and Jamie went to Stephen's house for a pre-game party. When I arrived at the spectator stands, Eileen was standing in a corner, crying her head off.

"Eileen, what's wrong? What's going on?" She wouldn't answer.

Then I saw Stephen. "Stephen, what's wrong with Eileen and where's Jamie?"

At first, he didn't answer. His eyes were cloudy and he looked mad. "Jamie took off with some guy," he said. "She and Eileen had a fight."

I went back to Eileen. "Eileen, talk to me. Tell me what happened."

"Jamie's mad at me. She and Stephen were talking and he tried to hit on her," Eileen blubbered. "He's supposed to be going out with you and that just made me mad." Eileen was crying harder now. "So I yelled at her and now she's upset. It's all Stephen's fault, Kayla. He's a jerk!"

I went back to Stephen and confronted him. At first he denied his actions, but he could tell I didn't believe him.

"Aw," he said. "I was just trying to see what her reaction would be. I'm sorry, okay? I didn't know it would upset you. I didn't mean anything by it! I'm sorry."

I didn't like what I was hearing. I didn't believe he could do that to Jamie, my friend, and then say what he did. We broke up for a day or two. But it wasn't long before he sweet-talked me into dating again. Over the next few days, he kept calling and apologized until I forgave him.

All that fall during my senior year, we went to parties together. He'd come over to my house and I'd go over to his. My Mom wouldn't let me entertain him when she and Ray weren't home, so we went to Stephen's house when his parents weren't there.

In the beginning, it was so innocent. We just sat around, watched television or videos and talked. It sounds so naive, but I didn't realize what was on his mind. He told me nothing would happen and I trusted him. First we started kissing and laughing. Then everything got more serious.

In the beginning, I was scared. I didn't want to have sex. And yet I was curious. What was it like? I was afraid I might get pregnant, but he kept telling me it was all right . . . that nothing would happen. And I believed him. It couldn't happen to me.

I didn't plan for us to have sex. But it happened—more than once. I couldn't ask Mom about protection—birth control for me—because that would mean I had planned for sex to occur. And I knew she'd try to talk me out of it.

I knew Stephen had enlisted in the Marine Corps, but I didn't know he was leaving for basic training on November 28. He didn't tell me until about the second week of that month. It would be a long time before I'd see him again.

The day Stephen left, we both cried. For days afterward, I was depressed. At first, when he got there, he wrote me twice a week. He would say, "I love you, I miss you, and I can't wait to get home." I thought that was really nice. I lived for those letters. But I didn't know that I was pregnant or that his whole attitude toward me would change once the news was broken to him. I only knew I loved him.

My first letter from him came only four days after he had left. It described what it was like to be in basic training. He said he was stiff and sore from exercises. His letters were filled with four-letter words. I think he was trying to be funny, but instead, he sounded immature and foul-mouthed. He ended the first letter with:

". . . Well, I gotta run, honey . . . I've been thinking of you often lately. I love you, Kayla! . . .and you'd better wait for me, you original sinner."

In November, Mom had resigned from her position at WQAD-TV. There had been managerial changes and she wasn't happy working there anymore. She began to look at her career and felt the need for a change. After much soul-searching, and discussing opportunities with area experts, she decided to open a designer dress shop.

Shortly after Stephen left Davenport, I made an appointment at the Maternal Health Center. I knew I should do something about birth control before he came back home on leave.

I kept my appointment, had the physical examination and filled a prescription for birth control pills. I was told to start taking them after my next period.

It never came . . . .

By the beginning of December I started suspecting I might be pregnant. In other parts of the world, thousands of people were dying from a toxic gas leak at a Union Carbide insecticide plant. Stacy Keach had pleaded guilty to importing cocaine into Britain and started serving a nine-month jail sentence. At home, the Davenport School system had announced plans to pass a $10 million bond referendum. But nothing going on in the world mattered to me. I was consumed with thoughts of pregnancy.

Day after day, I was really sick. Several times, I had to go home early from work at the department store. One day I went to the drugstore and bought an EPT kit, a self-testing system for pregnancy. It came out positive. Still I tried to tell myself, "This can't be true." So I didn't believe it.

I couldn't tell Mom. I still hoped it was the flu—that I'd wake up and this terrible dream would be over. Instead, every morning was like yesterday's. I had morning sickness and it lasted all day long.

Jamie tried to be helpful when I told her about my pregnancy on the telephone. She had tears in her voice. She said, "Kayla, You know you can get an abortion in Iowa City."

"I don't know. I don't think I can do that."

I believe abortion is wrong. I couldn't end the life of my own flesh and blood. I knew Jamie didn't favor abortion either. She was grasping at solutions to the problem and was willing to help me no matter what I decided. She said she felt so helpless, but she didn't know what else to say. She told me she wasn't angry with me, but she was mad at Stephen.

I was indignant when Jamie told her mother what I had said to her in confidence. But I could understand why she did. She's really close to her Mom and she talks to her about everything. I couldn't help wondering if she would have told her mother if *she* had been the one who was pregnant.

Together at a pay telephone booth, Jamie and I tried to call Stephen to tell him I thought I was pretty sure I was pregnant. I didn't want him to hear it from me in a cold, shocking letter. But it's hard to reach someone in boot camp. After we dialed the number, we were told you could only talk with a Marine in training by calling Red Cross, and it needed to be an emergency. (I thought this was an emergency!) Besides that, you had to be a relative.

Thinking fast, we decided to lie, saying Jamie and I were in a car accident. When Stephen heard the message, he called his parents! We didn't hear anything for days. When he wrote, he blamed Jamie for the call and said he was punished for it. We didn't believe it. He was just trying to make us feel guilty.

A few days later, I wrote to Stephen and told him my suspicions. In the back of my mind, I half hoped he cared enough about me to offer to marry me. I wasn't sure that's what I wanted, but I wanted him to prove himself to be a responsible, caring human being. My letter started a flurry of responses, but I didn't always like what I was reading.

It was Christmas Eve when I told Eileen. I had missed a week of school and been in bed the whole time. Eileen, a good friend for four years, came to deliver a Christmas present and we exchanged gifts. Her reaction matched Jamie's exactly.

"You can't be. No way." she said. Her face was full of shock and disbelief. It was as if my news had taken the joy of Christmas from her.

She started to cry and, walking to my side, she gave me a warm hug. She sat on the edge of the bed, close to me.

"Well, what are you going to do?" she asked. "Whatever you do, don't get an abortion."

I said, "No, I can't do that." I knew Eileen was adamant against abortion. She's really emotional about teen pregnancies.

"How are you going to tell your Mom, Kayla?" she asked.

I said, "I don't know." I felt so small when Eileen started to cry again.

"Kayla, I don't want to leave you alone tonight. But I can't stay. I have to go. My family is going to Midnight Mass."

I was sorry to see her go. I was sad that I couldn't attend Midnight Mass. It would be the first one I'd miss in ten years. Later, I found out she went home and told her Mom too. It seemed like everyone's mother knew I was pregnant but my own.

I was confused, miserable and worried sick. All the time I stayed in bed, I tried to decide what to do. I didn't have the courage to tell Mom. I knew it would affect her even more than it affected me. She had been a social worker who lived with pregnant and troubled teens. She had done a series on teenage pregnancies for the television station. Mom had always told me if I ever had any problems to come and talk to her, but I couldn't bring myself to go to her with this one.

On December 25th, when I was too sick to enjoy Christmas, I received a letter from Stephen in San Diego, California. He wrote saying he was almost ready for inspection, then it was to the rifle range and "we'll be out in the wilderness." He told me he was punished for our long-distance call about the car accident but I didn't believe it. Even then, I knew he often stretched the truth.

"You can write me but I'll only get the letters on Sunday. You'll probably only get 1 or 2 letters from me about 'our' problem. I think you know what the decision has to be, even though it may be wrong. I'd lose my Quality Ending Program (advance rank) and you couldn't go to school or work. You can't wait until I get paid (2 months) so just figure something out. I'm not worried, you're a smart girl. Just please don't say anything to anybody or my military career will take a giant step backward to nothing. Well, gotta go drill, then pack. I'll write in 2 days for sure (a long letter!) Bye Bye, Have faith."

Love,
Stephen

(the ####### car accident)
I got punished for that.
I know it was
Jamie's fault.

His letters frustrated me and made me angry. I was so disgusted with him. How could he be so insensitive to write such a thing when he knew I was pregnant with his child! I still loved him, but any hopes of spending my life with him began to dim. I was finally beginning to see his true personality. His normal "sweet-talk" wasn't there anymore; he left an entirely different impression on paper.

Later that Christmas Eve, just as I had for days, I stayed in bed. My door was closed, but I could hear Mom and Ray entertaining guests. Outside the weather was icy and more snow was predicted. It was supposed to be a season of joy and celebration and I just wanted to bury my head under my pillow and die. So many times, I thought of running away. I hated disappointing everyone and burdening them with my problems.

"Kayla has the flu," I heard Mom explain. "She's been sick for days and can't keep anything down. If she's not better by day after tomorrow, I'm taking her to the doctor."

"It's a shame to be so sick over Christmas," a woman's voice answered. "It must have put a 'damper' on your whole Christmas."

"It has, but that's not what's important," Mom responded. "I'm worried about Kayla."

I felt so awful. I was filled with guilt for being sick and maybe pregnant, and more guilty about ruining my family's Christmas. And I was angry at Stephen for doing this to me . . . and not caring enough to be responsible for his actions and to help me. It wasn't all my fault that this had happened. But I was the one suffering for it.

Mom came into my room that Christmas Eve after the guests had left.

"If you're not better in the next couple of days, we're going to take you to the doctor." Mom's voice was calm and soothing, but her words had a chilling effect on me. I pulled the covers closer to my chin and shuddered.

"Can you eat anything?" she asked. She brushed my hair back from my eyes.

"I'd like to have a chocolate shake." It was the only thing I could imagine that would taste good.

"We don't have any ice cream. I'll ask Ray to go buy one for you." She smiled and there was momentary comfort in her expression.

We talked a few moments more, then she said good-night and left. As she walked through the door, panic gripped me. I felt so scared! I kept telling myself, I'm going to get better. I'm not going to throw up anymore. I'm not going to be sick anymore . . . but it didn't work. Just then, I had to run to the bathroom and vomit.

The chocolate shake tasted good, but my health didn't improve and Mom made the appointment with the family doctor.

As she drove, Mom looked straight ahead over the steering wheel and said, "Kayla, honey, do you think you know what's wrong with you?"

I clutched my hands in my lap and started to cry.

My mother's voice was sad. "Do you think you know, Kayla?"

"Yes," I said. I glanced at her out of the corner of my eye; her face had a pained expression. Her knuckles were white where she gripped the wheel.

"You're pregnant, aren't you?"

"I think so," I said, but my voice didn't sound like me. It sounded far away. That's where I wished I could be . . . far away.

"I thought so too," she whispered. "You haven't been yourself lately. I told Ray you were showing the same kind of symptoms I had when I was pregnant."

The doctor's office was clean, neat and foreign looking. The exam table was hard and uncaring. Even as I was being examined, I felt afraid and alone. The pregnancy test completed, we went home to wait for the results. When the phone rang, I couldn't answer it. I waited for Mom to pick up the receiver. I listened and watched until she put the phone back in the cradle.

She turned and looked at me. There were tears in her eyes. "The doctor said you're pregnant." I began to cry. My worst fears had been confirmed.

I cried forever it seemed like, but at least now I wasn't alone. I had been right; this situation hurt my Mom more than me . . . and it was hurting me a lot. We cried together.

It was so sad. Everyone who heard the news was heartbroken. A baby should be such joy—it was Mom's first grandchild. But instead of bringing happiness, it was if someone had died. Even Ray was grief-stricken. It was the first time I ever saw him cry.

My days were filled with confusion and TV soap operas. I kept imagining myself the beautiful woman in one of the starring roles: pregnant and unmarried. Right now, my own life *was* a soap opera.

After Christmas vacation, I didn't go back to Assumption High School. There was only one week before the end of the semester. In January, I started walking to classes at the Teen Academic and Parenting Program (T.A.P.P.), sponsored by the Davenport School system. I thought at least I would be with other girls in the same situation. It would make this whole journey easier. But I was wrong.

Everything seemed to keep getting worse.

5

Family Turmoil

The kitchen was like a pot filled with boiling tempers—five of them.

"Just leave me alone!" I shouted, hot with anger. I could feel my fingernails digging into my palms. "I don't want to talk about it. Why are you after me all the time?"

"You aren't eating," Mom yelled back. People told us I looked like my mother but I didn't think so. She always looked pretty and well-groomed.

"You're a mess. You haven't cleaned up for days."

"I don't feel good!" My voice broke and I wildly blinked back tears. "Why can't you just leave me alone?"

Until now, Corey, Aaron and Ray had stayed in the background. They knew better than to get involved in a fight between this mother and daughter.

"Calm down, you guys. We won't get anywhere if you keep shouting like this," Corey said. My oldest brother hated it when anyone raised their voice to someone else in the family. It happened so seldom that when it did, he got upset.

Tears rolled down my mother's cheeks. Just watching her made me feel worse. I still felt ill, like I had the flu. Over and over again, the same words flowed through my mind: *pregnant, baby, pregnant, baby.* The last thing I wanted to do was sit at the kitchen table and discuss my pregnancy with the family.

"It's all my fault. It's all my fault," Mom sobbed. "If only I'd talked to you more. I should have given you birth control pills. I should have—"

My self-esteem was below rock bottom. I felt like an outcast in my own family. These people were all strangers, accusing me of sexual misconduct. I had been a bad girl and everywhere I looked, someone's eyes reminded me of it. It made me angry. I still loved Stephen and I wanted my relationship with him to be special. I didn't want the whole world to condemn it or me.

But that was what was happening.

"No, it's not your fault, Mom," I protested. "I would've done it anyway." I couldn't look at anyone and my clammy hands were clutched in my lap. A cold sweat broke out on my back. I felt so awful. Once Mom had been sick physically and emotionally—she'd eaten baby food for weeks. Now I knew how it felt to suffer from a similar illness of the body and spirit.

Corey and Aaron sat together, I was next to Mom, and Ray was on the other side of her. The kitchen—brightly decorated with blue, green, and orange butterflies in a yellow field—was usually the coziest room in the house. I looked past Petey in his birdcage toward the greenhouse. It was filled with blooming geraniums and healthy tropical plants.

Everywhere I looked, there were signs of new life. Everything I looked at reminded me that a baby was growing in me.

And I was miserable.

"Well, I feel responsible for not teaching you right from wrong. If it isn't my fault, why did it happen?" Mom asked. "Tell me why it happened, Kayla. I want to try to understand."

"Why can't you just leave me alone? Why do you have to keep harping at me? I'll eat more when I feel better. Right now, all I want is to go back to bed."

Mom wasn't about to let me run away and hide. If she had ever preached anything to us, it was to be responsible for our actions. If one of us broke something, there was no point in trying to run from punishment.

"What do you expect me to think, Kayla? You act like you're mad at me." She bit down hard on her lower lip to stop it from quivering. "You won't eat, you won't talk to me, you're unbearable to live with. What am I supposed to do with you?"

Corey's voice was inflamed and belligerent. "If Stephen ever shows his face at this house again, I'll punch him out. How could he do this and then just take off?"

His statement gave me mixed emotions. I was upset Corey would do that to Stephen, but at the same time I was proud of my brother for defending me.

"Corey, stay out of it," I said hotly.

"What are we going to tell our friends?" Aaron asked. "My sister is pregnant?" He acted like it hadn't sunk in yet. "What will everyone think?"

Ray hadn't said anything. It was as if he was waiting for the storm to pass before dealing with the aftermath. Emotions were so high, he knew he couldn't help at this point. So he let us say what we had to say. His face took on a pained look when he glanced at Mom. I could tell her feelings were hurting him too.

Mom started to cry again and tried to control it. She dabbed her eyes with another tissue and took a deep breath. She began to explain to my brothers some of the changes that were taking place.

"Kayla will be going to classes at T.A.P.P.," she said. "That's a program sponsored by the Davenport School system. It stands for Teen Academic and Parenting Program. She'll finish high school in May and have the baby sometime in late August." She swallowed, blinking hard.

"If your friends say anything," she said to Aaron, "I expect you to be honest, but kind. You don't have to apologize because this happened. It happened and we have to deal with it. Kayla is still your sister."

I couldn't stand it any longer. I pushed my chair back, ran to my room and slammed the door.

The rest of Christmas vacation was miserable. I spent most of my time in bed, watching soap operas: *All My Children, One Life to Live* and *General Hospital*. I told my friend, Madge, that I was pregnant and now all of my close girlfriends knew about it. It was funny how easy they fixed life's problems when they happened on the soaps.

One day after school, Madge, Eileen and Jamie came to visit. We closed the door to my bedroom and talked.

"Everyone is asking about you," Jamie said. "I keep telling them you're sick. I don't want to lie."

"Kayla, what shall we tell people at school?" Madge asked. "Everyone wants to know when you are coming back to classes."

At first, I didn't know what to tell them.

"I don't want it to get around just yet," I said. "It will spread like wildfire, once it gets out. Maybe you could say I have 'mono' or something." Mononucleosis, an infectious glandular illness characterized by fever, sore throat and swollen lymph glands, occasionally affected teenagers who over-extended themselves. At least the symptoms were partly right. I was getting a lot of bedrest these days and I certainly had a swelling.

Jamie, Eileen and Madge couldn't keep my secret forever. Once it broke, the news spread fast via the grapevine—to every corner of the earth, it seemed to me. They said everyone reacted the same way: "Kayla? Sweet, innocent, quiet Kayla? She would never do a thing like that." They couldn't believe I would care about someone enough to want to make love. To them, I was still innocent.

I felt like I had leprosy. There were some blessings, I guess. I didn't have to face all of those people and watch them look down to my stomach to see if I was showing yet. Still, I missed being with my friends and attending classes at Assumption. I couldn't contain my curiosity. Every day I questioned one of the girls: did anyone ask about me?

After New Year's Day, I was still too sick to go back to Assumption. The semester ended on January 11 without me, much to my disappointment. It didn't help the state of my health that I hadn't heard anything from Stephen. If it hadn't been for Jamie, Eileen and Madge, I would have felt totally isolated.

Mom and I visited T.A.P.P. (pronounced Tapp) a few days before the new semester began. We talked with Mrs. McCoy who was in charge of the program. I was still sick and I was scared out of my wits. Together the three of us planned classes so I could graduate: American literature, English composition, cooking and typing. Mrs. Brown, the counselor, gave us a tour of the classrooms. Later she told me I looked more humiliated by my pregnancy than anyone she had ever met. She said she felt so sorry for me when I turned away from them to face the wall.

On the first floor, not far from the nursery, were two bulletin boards on the wall. The first one had horizontal pockets arranged by month. In almost every one, there were slips of paper with a student's "due" date, or date of delivery.

The other board was filled with construction-paper bunnies. Each contained the name of mother and her newborn baby, with measurements. Very few of these names would change, Mrs. Brown explained, because so many of the mothers were keeping their babies. Adoptive parents usually picked a new name.

A strange feeling swept through my body. Soon my name would be in the pocket for August because that was when my baby was due to be born. Since I planned to release my baby, she would be renamed.

"In the school year 1986-87, six girls planned to release their babies," said Mrs. Brown. "But only four ended up doing so. This year, three have relinquished their babies and one more is definitely planning to. Another girl is talking about it. That's not very many when you consider we average between 50 and 70 students each year."

On Tuesday, January 22, 1985, it was another first day at a new school for me. I was amazed by the differences I saw between Assumption and T.A.P.P. It was awful because there were no guys, just girls— and they were all pregnant. Some were only seventh and eighth graders! That really shocked me!

I didn't show until my seventh month so all the time I kept saying to myself, "I don't belong here." I guess I had been pretty sheltered at a private Catholic school. Here there were black girls as well as whites. Lots of the expectant mothers looked like huge, sloppy "couch potatoes" in sweat pants and t-shirts. They made no effort to hide their big stomachs.

Almost no one wore frilly maternity tops or nice clothes and some of the girls scared me. They were loud, fought with each other and some of them talked stupid most of the time, I thought. I couldn't believe it when I heard of one girl who was pregnant with her third baby. She was younger than I was! There was another girl whose mother's boyfriend had gotten her pregnant. No wonder I was shocked. If this was the real world, I didn't like it much. Now, I felt out-of-place everywhere—Assumption and here.

That first day, I ran into a girl I had known from early days at Assumption. I was seated and saw her first when she walked into class. My heart started beating faster. I said, "Oh, no!" and put my elbows on my desk, burying my face in my hands. I was so embarrassed.

"Kayla! What are you doing here?" she asked when she recognized me.

"What do you think, Heather?" I answered. When I looked up, her face was filled with surprise.

"What are you doing here?" I asked even though I already knew the answer.

"What do you think, Kayla?" she responded with a sad smile.

After that, we spent most of our free time together. But there was one difference. Heather planned to keep her baby. So she took the class in infant nurturing. I had decided I would probably release my baby for adoption. Since that class met the first thing in the morning, I didn't go to school until ten o'clock.

When the other students asked me what I planned to do about the baby, I told them I thought I would release it for adoption. I planned to go on to college. It was so hard at T.A.P.P. because everyone there was keeping her baby. Both Cathies that I ran around with, and Heather . . . .Some of the other girls didn't like me because they were keeping their babies and knew I was giving mine up for adoption.

I didn't even think of myself as being pregnant. I kept telling myself, "It's not going to be any big deal. I'm going to be able to give her up for adoption."

"I don't know how you can do that," one girl said. "It's your baby. How can you give it away? I would never do that."

"Well, I'm not sure what I'll do, but when the time comes, I'll decide," I answered, looking away. I didn't want to talk about it. I didn't think it was anyone else's business—especially if they weren't one of my friends. It was my decision. But mostly I didn't want to talk about it with strangers.

"It's going to be hard, Kayla," one of my friends told me. "You're going to see her and you'll want to keep her."

I said, "No, I think I'll be all right."

One girl tried to talk me into keeping my baby. She said if I did, we could share an apartment together. I told her I didn't know if that would work or not.

Mrs. Brown counseled me about adoption. She asked me questions, trying to make me open up, but I couldn't tell her how I really felt. She tried to prepare me for criticism from others, and about the feelings I could expect.

"I get so angry with people who say adoption is the easy way out," she said. "Anyone who says this is wrong. Often it takes more courage to release a baby than to keep it."

When I left her office, I went to the first floor and walked past the nursery. It was as if I were drawn to the door, but I didn't go in unless I was with Heather. Babies cried, sprawling in the rows of cribs, begging to be picked up, fed, changed or just cuddled. In the five months I attended classes at T.A.P.P., I probably went into that room only twice, and then it was because Heather was in there.

Every day when I arrived home from classes, I checked the mail for a letter from Stephen. Day after day, I was disappointed. Before I told him I was pregnant, he had written twice a week. It made me so angry. I kept thinking, how could he do that? How could he father our child and then not even write to me!

On the last day of the month, he sent a letter. It was full of apologies and excuses for not writing. He criticized me for not being more understanding.

"—as I was saying, I really am sorry about the whole unfortunate ordeal but there's not much we can do now but get it over with and be done with it. If my parents haven't already told you, (which I'm sure they have), Adoption is the only way to resolve the situation—THE ONLY! You want to do something else, hey, it's all yours to try to do it—just leave me out—I know that sounds selfish, but adoption is the only way in my mind.

". . . There had better not be anybody ready to jump on my back when I get home, or STAND BY! . . . Don't expect me to be all ready to jump into the situation. . . . I'm sorry about it all. Honestly. Back to the real life in Davenport, Iowa—BASKET-

BALL? I hear the Hawkeyes are 16-4 and that West is kicking some ###.....

"A little something to dwell on—our little saying before we sit down for class or dinner-chow. Drill Instructor says 'Ready!' we say—

"Born on a mountain
Raised in a cave,
Humping and fighting is all we crave—

"Then the D.I. would say, 'Sit.' Then we would yell 'Kill, rape, eat dead babies' (as we were sitting). Beautiful, isn't it. I know you don't think so."

No, I didn't think so and neither did my girlfriends when I showed them the letter. If I had known he wouldn't write again until mid-March, I should have been glad. His letters weren't helpful or supportive; they only made me feel worse. But of course, I wanted Stephen to write. I wanted him to tell me he cared about me and the baby he had helped create, but he didn't, and I'll never forgive him for that.

The next week, Mom called Stephen's recruiting officer and asked him what could be done to make Stephen help pay expenses for my delivery and hospitalization. She said they talked a long time. Then she told me to call the officer. I did and he seemed nice. He acted like he cared about what had happened to me. Later, Stephen talked to him and "told him off," suggesting he mind his own business.

Mom was cutting up fruit for her lunch when I walked into the kitchen. It was early morning before I went to school. She didn't have to be at the dress shop until nine-thirty.

"Kayla, we called Stephen's parents and set up a meeting," Mom said. "They're coming over here on Wednesday night. I want you to be here."

I felt the blood draining from my face. My heart seemed to stop beating. I didn't want to have to face Stephen's parents.

"Why do I have to be here?" I asked. My voice was just a whisper. "I don't have anything to say."

"It's because of you that we're meeting. This is their grandchild, too," Mom said, her voice thick with emotion. "All of us are affected by this pregnancy. And it's your responsibility to be a part of the discussion." Her statement shocked me. I hadn't thought about this baby being the Webster's grandchild too.

Mom was sympathetic to my feelings, but unrelenting.

Stephen's parents came to the house about the middle of February. It was really hard to look at them. I knew Stephen's parents really liked me a lot and I thought they were good people. But it was so embarrassing to face them.

While I sat there, looking at the floor with my hands clasped between my knees, they talked to each other. I felt like I had a huge scarlet letter, "A," branded on my back.

"We lived in Scotland. That was where Stephen was born," his mother explained. "We adopted him before we moved back to the United States. He's never wanted to find his real parents."

I almost laughed. Stephen had told me his real parents were killed in a plane wreck. That's why he was adopted as a baby. He had lied to me about that too. Couldn't he tell me the truth about anything?

"Stephen was illegitimate, too," his mother said softly.

A shudder ran through me. I hate that word, I thought. It's such an old, ugly word. Why doesn't someone throw that word out?

"I was in the service myself—the Marines," Stephen's father said, picking up the conversation. "It's good training."

In the end, they talked just about me. I imagined the "A" on my back growing like Pinocchio's nose. In the story, Pinocchio kept lying and his nose grew longer. As these adults talked about me, the deeper and hotter my shame and embarrassment grew. I had stared at the floor for so long, I could have totaled the threads in the carpet.

Ray said, "One mistake has been made. They don't need to make another by getting married."

I had thought about marriage. Before I found out I was pregnant, Stephen had talked about being stationed in Hawaii. He'd said he'd send for me and we'd be together. As soon as I discovered I was pregnant, there was no more talk of Hawaii. I didn't tell anyone, but there was a time I imagined being on a beach blanket with our baby next to me.

I remembered Mom's and Ray's wedding a few years ago. It was such a celebration. I had dreamed of my own wedding, but now that I was pregnant, I couldn't imagine a special occasion. No, I didn't want to get married. At least I didn't think I did.

"Well, I guess the best thing to do is to give the baby up for adoption," Stephen's mother said.

"Kayla, what do you think about this?" Mom asked.

I just shrugged. I didn't know what to think about this. I wished the floor would open up and swallow me . . . and never spit me back up.

After a few more minutes, they started to leave. As they went out the door, Stephen's mother looked back at me. She smiled weakly and said, "Keep in touch."

But I could tell she didn't mean it.

Every day in classes, I went through the motions and watched for the hands on the clock to roll around to four. All I wanted to do was go home. It wasn't that I was bored. I always had something to do. It's just that I didn't want to be at T.A.P.P. I knew about all the things I was missing at Assumption. It was my senior year and I hated not being a part of the fun.

Jamie, Eileen and Madge tried to make me go places—to parties and movies—but I still didn't feel good. The smell of perfume nauseated me—even expensive perfume like Giorgio. It was awful to get into a car where several females were wearing different scents. Finally I asked my friends to go easy on the fragrances. When it wasn't perfume, food nauseated me.

I had always hated smoking, but now it really bothered me. When I finally went to a party, everything and everyone there unintentionally bothered me. The smells—beer, pizza, perfume, aftershave, cigarette smoke—sent my stomach into somersaults. The loud music made my head ache. It seemed as though I had changed a lot in the last few months.

I knew I was kidding myself. There was more to it than physical discomfort. I didn't want to face anyone I knew. These people had all been my friends. Now it seemed as if I didn't have a face. All eyes were focused on my stomach.

In February and March, I started suntan treatments. I was so sickly-looking after losing weight and being ill for so long . . . and the dermatologist couldn't give me medicine for my skin any longer because it would harm the baby. He suggested I might try indoor suntanning.

One day, not long before a visit to my father's home in Florida, I came home from a treatment and said to my younger brother, Aaron, "Look how gorgeous I'm getting from suntanning."

He wasn't impressed. "No one's going to be looking at that on the beach, silly. They'll all be looking at your fat stomach."

Hot tears stung my eyes. I knew he hadn't meant to hurt my feelings, but I felt like I'd been hit with a wet dishrag. Every time I forgot about the baby and tried to feel good about myself, the reality of my pregnancy re-surfaced to bring me back to earth.

One night while Corey was getting ready to go out on a date, I heard Ray call to him. "Corey, I want to talk to you." They didn't know I was eavesdropping.

Ray asked Corey where he was taking his date, and what time he'd be home. Yes, he had enough money and he'd be careful with the car.

"Corey, you can see how all of this business with Kayla has hurt your mother," he said, getting to the point. "I want you to learn from the mistakes that have been made. If there's one lesson in all of this for you, it's this: 'When you go out on a date, for Heaven sakes, keep your fly zipped!'"

6

Innocent Revenge

He acted like he didn't know me.

In March, Stephen was on leave from boot camp, the first time he'd been home since we said tearful good-byes at the airport. I didn't know he was home until Jamie saw him at the shopping mall. I couldn't believe he didn't call! It was bad enough that I didn't hear from him. But then our parents set up a meeting for all of us at Stephen's house.

I dreaded going to the meeting but I was glad I still didn't show much. I didn't want to see Stephen again while looking like a balloon. I'd started wearing oversized blouses and maternity slacks—they were more comfortable. I was more accepting of my role as a pregnant woman and I decided I might as well be comfortable. But I didn't want stretch marks so I spent hours slathering on tons of lotion to help keep the skin supple. As time passed, morning sickness was affecting me less and less.

From the time the meeting was set up, until it actually occurred, I worried about it. I hadn't seen Stephen for so long, and I knew we had both changed—at least physically. He wrote of long hours of exercise and weight loss. And instead of losing weight like he had, I had gained.

On the scheduled meeting date, Stephen's mother and their big, ugly dog met us at the front door. We walked up the stairs of the small split-foyer home into the living room.

It looked more picked up than I remembered from my dates with Stephen. After all, we hadn't expected anyone to come into the house then. The couch was covered with a blue bedspread and there were dog hairs all over the furniture. Traffic patterns showed in the soiled, green carpet. This home—unlike ours—didn't have artwork or expensive wallhangings anywhere. Instead of weeping fig trees or palms that reached toward the ceiling, there were plastic flowers in a vase on the table.

Stephen's hair was cut so short it shocked me. But even with his haircut, I thought he was really muscular and handsome. I stared at him and he looked back. Then he smiled nervously and looked away. He shifted his weight back and forth. As if to cover up for his part in the situation, he squared his shoulders and arched his back, acting as if he didn't care.

How many times had I imagined what it would be like to see him again? I expected this person who meant so much to me to offer a hug, or a warm, loving smile . . . . When he greeted me, he just said, "Hi." I hoped it was because our parents were standing around.

We sat down and for the next hour and a half, he all but ignored me while our parents dominated the conversation. They small-talked for a while, about the weather and the news, saying nothing, just filling the silence. I could hardly breathe. Tension stifled the air. I clasped my hands and placed them between my knees. I noticed I had a scratch on one hand, and my polish on one fingernail was chipped. Out of the corner of my eye, I could see Stephen's eyes on me and I burned with embarrassment. I pulled my blouse out, letting it fall against my body.

Mom's soft voice pierced my thoughts when she asked Stephen how he liked the military.

"Oh, it's great," he said. "I can't wait to get back to California. Then I'm looking forward to being stationed in Hawaii. You see, now I know that everywhere I go around here, there are 'Unsat Civilians,'" he explained politely. "That means they're unsatisfactory people compared to the Marines personnel. Everyone does as they please. It's not that way in the service. The Marines is the best place in the world to be."

I wanted to be sick. Who was this stranger? My stomach felt queasy. I wasn't sure if it was my pregnancy or because of what I was hearing. When Stephen mentioned Hawaii, it reminded me of the promises he had made to send for me.

Now he couldn't look me in the eye.

Finally, our parents got around to the point of the visit.

"Well, I suppose we should talk about what we came to discuss," Mom said.

She told them I would deliver in late August and that they expected Stephen to help with the medical expenses. I was anxious to see how the father of my child would react to that news.

When I looked up, Stephen was nodding his head like a fishing bobber on the water! "Yes, that's fine," he continued to say.

Inside, I began to seethe with anger. He acted as if it were no big deal that I was carrying his child. I couldn't believe my eyes or ears. As far as he was concerned, this seemed to be no big deal. I couldn't believe it!

The conversation seemed to last forever. The pregnancy, delivery, medical and legal matters were thoroughly exhausted. Stephen sat through a lecture on responsibility, and I had to hear that his parents thought I was trying to trap their precious son into marriage. My face burned and I could've crawled under the distasteful carpet.

My head felt light. How I wished I could go back in time to a year ago! The tension hadn't eased in the whole time we were here and I would have given anything to avoid the unpleasant scene. I wanted to breathe again . . . the clean, fresh air of innocence.

* * *

As raindrops fell softly around us, Jamie and I crept toward the Webster's through the dark. A car drove by, casting light on this street where we wanted only darkness. What if we were caught? They could press charges.

"Jamie, do you see anyone?" I whispered.

"No, it's okay. Everyone in the house must be asleep. Let's get to work."

I giggled and it helped relieve the tension. When I looked at Jamie— the friend everyone said looked like me—she put her hand to her mouth to stifle her giggles. Her eyes danced with mischief and excitement.

It was 12 A.M. and all of our planning had been targeted to exactly this moment. In our hands we carried rolls of toilet paper, several cans of shaving cream, about six eggs we stole from Jamie's refrigerator and a large container filled with little curls of styrofoam packing material.

When we reached the house, we set our packages down and began. Scattering styrofoam all over the green grass of the Webster's home, Jamie's smile widened in approval. "It looks like popcorn," she said. "That'll show the crumbly."

I laughed at Jamie's use of the word, crumbly. It was the worst thing she could say to describe someone she didn't like.

Next, Jamie broke the seal on the toilet paper and handed me a roll. I smiled, feeling so close to her. We were "partners in crime."

There was a big grin on her face as the rain fell softly like mist on the dark night. We started stringing the pink tissue all over the bushes and trees—everywhere we could reach. While we worked, Jamie giggled. It was contagious . . . it felt so good. Stephen was still home on leave and he hadn't called me once. I was carrying his child and tonight—this very evening—I knew he was probably out with another girl.

We smashed the eggs in our hands instead of throwing them at the house. We were afraid of waking anyone inside, or the neighbors. We spread the sticky mess on the wall.

After that dreadful meeting, I was filled with a desire for revenge. When Jamie and I first started scheming, Jamie had wanted to use spray paint on the house, but I had said no. "Shaving cream will be good enough," I said. "He'll get the message."

Now, as I shook one can, Jamie put her hands on her hips and smiled broadly at me with a look of satisfaction. I had told her about the meeting at his parents' home. She had become indignant with anger and righteousness.

"He's such a crumbly," she said over and over. "He's nothing but a crumbly and I hate him for what he did to you."

Jamie's light brown hair was mussed and damp from the rain, but her face glowed. It felt so good to be here with her. The air tasted fresh and clean; it seemed to wash away my anger and problems, even if only temporarily.

Popping the cap, I tested the foam on my hand, and began to write on the side of the house. I could smell the lime fragrance. The roof and gutter protected the shaving cream and egg from the rain.

Slowly, I spelled each letter in huge, sweeping motions, thoughtlessly writing the words that burned on my heart: U—N—S—A—T L—A— I—R. I remembered the word "Unsat" from the meeting. Unsat. That's what *he* is: an unsatisfactory individual. He used me and lied to me. He said he loved me. I didn't believe that any more.

I couldn't understand why he lied to me about his past, about his being adopted and his parents being killed in a plane crash. What if my baby was a boy? Would he someday lie about his beginnings? I hoped not. I wanted my baby to know I loved him.

The shaving cream formed unevenly on the wall, but I thought the letters were perfect. One can was empty and I handed it to Jamie. She gave me the second one. I shook it, popped the cap and started to underscore the word U-N-S-A-T. With the release of pressure from the can, there was a release for me. This was sweet revenge . . . .

"Kayla, there's a car coming!" Jamie said in a loud whisper. "Maybe it's them. Maybe they aren't asleep. Let's get out of here!"

I stifled an urge to scream. "I'm finished. Let's go."

Clutching the can, I began to run across the back yard with Jamie, through the wet grass along the side of the house toward the wooden fence. I struggled to climb over it and a chunk separated from the top. "You broke it!" Jamie said, laughing.

Jamie's car was parked on the next street over and I felt like I was running a long-distance marathon. I was so scared we'd be caught!

My friend was already way ahead of me. I was afraid to run too hard because of the baby. "Hurry, Kayla!"

"Jamie, wait. I can't keep up."

I giggled nervously, feeling giddy with excitement. This was the most fun I'd had since before I'd learned I was pregnant. I felt so good, so free, running through the rain and the dark night—lit only by a distant street light. I was running as if in a dream . . . it was as if there were something after me.

Suddenly, I slipped on loose rock in the alley and fell face down in the mud. The gravel scraped my face and I was covered with mud, but I didn't give it a second thought.

"The baby . . ." I said out loud.

Jamie ran back to help me. Her face was full of concern as our eyes met. Her brows furrowed and her mouth was set in a thin line. She didn't know what to say and neither did I.

The tense silence made the night seem blacker than it was. As Jamie grabbed my elbow to help me up, a door slammed in the distance.

"Are you okay, Kayla?" she whispered with fear in her voice. "Do you feel anything?"

I shook my head no. "I think it's all right," I answered. "Let's get out of here."

Once we were back in the car, I put my hand on my stomach. I still wasn't very big yet, but I had felt life. It always startled me when the baby moved, as if rolling over in its sleep. It was like the fluttering of butterflies.

Jamie drove me to her home where I had planned to spend the night. We went into the house and down to the basement, where we hurriedly washed out my muddy clothes and hung them up to dry.

I later climbed under the blanket on the sectional and lay there grinning, staring at the ceiling and thinking of Stephen. I imagined him coming home on his motorcycle, seeing the soaked, dripping toilet paper on the bushes and trees, the smashed eggs and the little curls of styrofoam and the message on the protected wall. I laughed softly to myself. "That'll show him who's 'Unsat.'"

Smiling, I fell asleep.

* * *

The next day, Sunday, I went to Mass early. After I became pregnant, I continued to attend Mass, but I really didn't like to go because I felt everyone was staring at my stomach. And I felt so guilty. What was it Stephen had called me? Oh yes, the original sinner.

When I did go, I often lit a candle for my baby. I was surprised to discover that I prayed more now. Sometimes when I was alone in my room, I prayed for the baby . . . and for me.

That afternoon, while Mom and Ray were working at the new store, I was lounging around the house when the telephone rang. I was upstairs; Corey and Aaron were downstairs in the rec room watching a football game. I beat them to the phone. When I heard the familiar voice, I was glad I had. Anyone else might have said something rude and hung up.

Stephen didn't waste any time.

"Did you have fun last night, Kayla?" Stephen asked. "I know you did it."

"What?" I said, as I smiled from ear to ear and fought to keep from giggling. "What are you talking about?"

"Don't play dumb with me. I know you did it." I could hear his fingers drumming the kitchen counter.

"Did what? I don't know what you're talking about."

"You did it. I know you did. You even misspelled 'liar'," he said. His voice was calm and self-assured.

That stopped me. I knew how to spell "liar," all right. It constantly paraded through my thoughts.

"Stephen, what are you talking about? I don't have the faintest—"

"My dad saw you. He was out walking the dog—"

That did it. I gave in and started laughing. "Your dad didn't see anything," I said. "You couldn't tell the truth to save your life. No one walks the dog at that time of night."

He ignored my insult.

"I knew you did it. Who else? You and Jamie?" he asked. "I just hosed down the house and the shaving cream took the paint off."

For a minute I didn't say anything. My thoughts said "Uh oh." But out loud, my reaction was different. "I don't believe you. I don't believe anything you say anymore."

Weeks later, I received another letter from Stephen. It made me angry that he couldn't face me when he was home, but he could find time to write when he was bored or lonely.

March 10, 1985

Kayla,

Yes, believe it or not, I'm actually writing a letter. This is my 2nd since I've been here. Only you and my other girlfriend have the ultimate honor. I know, I know. I'm an irresponsible, self-centered, unsat individual. Sometimes I wonder if you're not right. At least in your case. Well, in any case, I'm sorry. I haven't been talking much to anybody, even at home. Enough of that.

So how are you doing, better I hope. You're still not getting sick, are you? (Now it's my turn to be sick, I've got one # # # # # # # stomach—intestinal infection that is more than discomforting, more like paralyzing. But that's another story.) I hope things are better for you though, you don't really deserve to go through 9 months of ####- ####. It would hamper you in shaving-creaming my house. (Just joking.) Does my wall still say UNSAT? Boy, I hope so.

So how are things at home? I hear the weather is pretty nice though. Maybe when I get back we can go back to our old trade of raking leaves. I hope it's warm when I get home so I can put on some shorts and jam around on the bike.

Things here are pretty cool, palm trees, sun, beach, crazy drives, lesbians and smog. It's just great. A bunch of us have gone to Los Angeles, Hollywood, Newport Beach and Dis-

neyland. Work is straining one's body, but I get off at 4:30.
And I also have weekends off so there's lots of time to enjoy
California life.

Well, I hope things are going O.K. for you and our parents.
Have some faith in me (if that's possible) until next time.

Love,
Stephen

I wrote back to him a few days later, telling him I couldn't believe
he had written. After the way he had treated me when he was on leave,
I didn't expect to hear from him again. By now I was so confused I
wasn't sure what I wanted to think of him. He had signed his letter,
"Love." Well, he didn't act like he loved me . . . or the baby. So why
had he bothered to write?

Frequently during my pregnancy, I asked my friend Madge if I could
visit her when she was babysitting for her tiny niece, Abby. I liked to
hold Abby and imagine what it would be like to feel my own baby in my
arms. I fed her, touched her soft skin, and felt a yearning deep within
me. What would Stephen's and my baby look like? Would it be a boy
or a girl? I secretly wanted a girl. Would she have his brown eyes and
hair? Or my lighter colored ones?

Toward the end of the month during spring break, I flew to visit my
father, Michael Becker, in Florida. He lived and worked there as a social worker. I had looked forward to it for so long and I had a great start
on a tan. Since I still wasn't showing that much and no one else knew
me there, I wore a two-piece bathing suit and basked in the warm out-
doors.

Dad didn't say much about my pregnancy. The only time he mentioned it, all he said was, "You're going to be okay, Kayla. Everything
will work out all right."

It was good to hear someone say that besides my mother. As the days and months of that long, awful winter became a part of my history, I grew more uncertain about the events to come.

I wasn't so sure everything would be okay.

7

No More Letters

Assumption High School decided to sponsor a spaghetti dinner where we could all dress up as clowns. It seemed appropriate since my whole life had become a multi-ringed circus. There were scheduled appointments with my counselor, obstetrician, the adoption lawyer . . . and my teachers. My friends asked me to go even though I was attending classes at T.A.P.P.

I didn't want to go to the dinner. I felt like an outsider. Everyone knew about me, and I was ashamed of what had happened. When people saw me, they always looked at my stomach to see if my pregnancy showed. I kept telling Eileen I wouldn't go, but then Mom said, "Kayla, just go. No one will be able to tell you're pregnant when you put on a clown costume."

That evening another friend, Kelly, Eileen, Madge and I were crowded into Eileen's bathroom, peering into the mirror, trying to draw faces on ourselves and each other. Kelly had been pregnant, delivered and kept her baby. She didn't have a costume so we put one together for her. Eileen had one of her own. I had borrowed a costume from Ray's sister and clown makeup from his niece. The wig was a mass of curls in yellow, green, orange and white. I wore a dunce cap-like hat with a pom pom on top. The costume concealed everything in a combination of one half white and the other half blue checks.

"Kayla, you need to put circles around your eyes like this. And more rouge on your cheeks," Eileen said.

"I don't know how to draw a face," I said and started laughing. Eileen and Kelly started laughing. It was as though I had pushed the first domino and all the others followed. We laughed so hard, tears came to my eyes. It felt so good!

After the spaghetti dinner at school, we went to a party. It was the first time I had been around kids from Assumption. They were coming up to me, asking how I was; I was surprised by their responses. It was the first time I felt more comfortable being out with people who knew me.

The next day, I had an appointment at four o'clock with the doctor. Early on in the pregnancy, I went about every five weeks. Now, as time drew near, the appointments were closer together. I hated it. I dreaded the exams, the invasion of my modesty—the doctor's probing, heavy-handed fingers. It was as if he didn't have time to be gentle.

I was worried about the bills I was running up and how I would pay them. Stephen was supposed to pay for half of the expenses; the doctor wanted money up front for prenatal care. But I had decided it would take the Marines to drag the money out of Stephen. He wasn't responsible enough to volunteer it.

At 3:45 P.M., I sat in the doctor's office, a small room with rust carpet and beige walls. Almost every magazine on the corner tables was for baby or child care: *Parents, Baby Talk* and *American Health.* The other alternative was—of all things—*Pinocchio.* It made me ache, to see so many magazine covers with healthy, beaming mothers and their perfect babies. I knew this should be a happy time for me, and yet this pregnancy was hurting so many people.

On the opposite wall, a young woman and man sat looking at a baby magazine together. Suddenly, she looked at the ceiling and twisted her head from side to side. The man spoke to her and she leaned forward. He began to massage her shoulders.

This scene made me ache, too. There was no one like that in my life to rub my shoulders, or my aching back. Their baby would have two parents to care about him.

I felt so alone. I wished Mom had come with me.

I went to Dr. Izetti's office faithfully because I knew prenatal care was important for my baby's well-being. A middle-aged with dark hair and brown eyes, Dr. Izetti was a brusque man. I could tell he didn't have much patience with unwed teen mothers. His voice rang with command when he ordered his nurses to take my blood pressure, weigh me, and check my urine. He looked for changes in the size of my uterus and measured me. He asked if there were any problems and, after I said no, he gave me a card with my next appointment on it.

Heather and I used to talk about listening to the baby's heartbeat. She described the first time she listened, and said her own heart skipped a beat, it was so incredible! My doctor never once asked me if I wanted to hear my baby's heartbeat. I never did get to hear it.

But I wanted this baby anyway. I wanted my baby to be healthy and happy—and to have all of the things I couldn't provide.

One day, I found out I wasn't the only one who wanted my baby.

Dr. Izetti wanted it, too.

After the exam, as I sat on the end of the table. He stood a few inches from the table, stared hard at me and said, "Do you know what you're going to do?" His voice was courteous yet patronizing.

I nodded. "I'm going through a private adoption with a lawyer."

He frowned. "Are you sure? I have a lot of couples who would like to have your baby."

He had mentioned this before, but this time it was different. He was more direct and looked me straight in the eye. I squirmed. I felt naked and defenseless even though I was fully dressed. I could feel tension in the room. My back ached and I longed to step down from the table. Again I wished Mom had come with me on this trip.

I leaned back to increase the distance between us, but he didn't move from the side of the table.

He went on to talk about how hard it was to find healthy, white babies for childless couples.

"Adoption is the best thing for you to do," he said. "You're making a wise choice. Then you can go on with your life. I have a long list of couples who would make wonderful parents for your child. Why don't you let me help you?"

I didn't know what to say. Tears welled up in my eyes. I wanted to answer him, to tell him off, but he was my doctor and I was afraid. I could feel his condescending attitude toward me and I didn't like it. His demeanor made me feel awful—like he thought I was a bad girl. But I remembered what Mrs. Brown, my counselor at T.A.P.P., always said, "There are no bad girls at T.A.P.P.—only pregnant ones."

When I didn't answer, he spoke. "Well, Kayla, won't you think about it?"

I didn't know what to say. I had already made my decision.

Disgruntled, he finally left the room. I stepped down and went out into the reception area. The nurse smiled at me from behind the counter and said, "Kayla, you know Dr. Izetti has lots of people who would like to have your baby."

"I know. He already told me." The blood began to pound in my temples; I was getting a headache.

As I was driving toward home, I cried. When I drove past Eileen in her parents' car, she saw me and followed. She pulled into the circle drive and got out of the car.

"Kayla, what's wrong?" she asked. I told her what had happened.

"They were pressuring me to let *them* make decisions for my baby," I protested. "I didn't like it."

"Don't worry, Kayla," she said. "Everything will be okay."

Later, at my mother's store, I told Mom about it. She wasn't surprised. "Oh, sure," she said. "A healthy white baby is worth a lot of money, about $10-$15,000 or more in some states. Of course he would like to have it. It means money for fees in his pocket."

I was disgusted and angry. I was glad I had already made my decision to call the adoption lawyer. At least I would have some control over my baby's future. If I allowed the doctor to take her, she would be gone to who knows whom or where? I knew what I wanted in an adoptive couple. I wanted to be able to say what kind of parents would raise her.

All along, I knew that after I gave up the baby for adoption, I would go on to college. So on a hot Saturday in April, I sat in a classroom at Central High School with students from all of the area high schools, squirming my way through the ACT test. It been part of my plans for a long time. I had to keep up my grades to get into college and the ACT tests were required for admission. I felt fat and awkward even though I didn't show much yet.

Some time ago, when Mom called the lawyer for me to schedule an appointment, he had told her, "It has to be Kayla's decision. It's her baby and she has to call me for an appointment herself." Weeks passed before I could muster the courage to call him again. I was still skeptical about giving up the baby, but I thought about my alternatives, looked up the number and made an appointment.

When I walked into his office for the first time on April 29, he sat behind his desk and talked softly to me. There were pictures of his family all around. He had two children, a boy and a girl. He led the conversation and I was glad to let him do it. As he asked questions about my due date, the name of the father, and so on, he took notes on a legal pad. Then he asked what kind of people I wanted for adoptive parents.

I smiled. I had thought about this a lot. Mom and I had discussed the potential parents in detail.

"I want a Catholic couple," I said. "They should be young and I don't want either of them to smoke. And I want the mother to stay home with my baby at least until he or she's in school."

He nodded, wrote everything down and then explained the procedures. He told me he had quite a few couples who wanted to adopt a child, but my criteria would help narrow the list.

"Are you sure you want to do this, Kayla?" he asked. "You need to be sure because if a couple becomes involved, there is heartbreak for them if you change your mind. I know this is difficult, but do you think this is really what you want to do?"

"Yes, I think so," I said.

This appointment left me feeling that I had made a good decision about going through a private adoption. I still had some doubts but I felt a little better.

All through April and May, life seemed mostly dull and monotonous. School on weekdays, and I stayed in my bedroom on weekends. I watched endless soap operas and read some. Lots of times, I thought about Stephen and tried to deal with my feelings of anger. Then I felt sorry for myself and wished this hadn't happen. Why did I listen to him when he said, "Nothing will happen. It'll be okay."

Toward the end of the school year, Jamie, Eileen and Madge tried to talk me into going out with them. I didn't want to go. I went with them to a basketball game or two, but I was self-conscious about what I looked like. That made me feel uncomfortable.

One night, Eileen called. "Kayla, let's go to a movie this weekend. It'll help you forget everything for a while."

"No, I think I'll just stay home. I don't feel too well." If I went to a movie, I knew I'd be uncomfortable sitting that long in a chair, and everything—smoke, perfume and even popcorn—still turned my stomach.

"Oh, come on, Kayla," she coaxed. "You can't hibernate for nine months. Let's go out and have some fun. Jamie and Madge are going with me. You come too."

"No. I don't want to go," I said sharply. "It's no fun for me like this."

There was silence at the other end. When Eileen spoke again, I could tell I had hurt her feelings. After a few moments, we said goodbye and hung up.

For the next day and a half, I felt guilty about snapping at Eileen. She didn't deserve it. She was trying to help me through this and I had hurt the feelings of one of my best friends. When I couldn't stand it any longer, I called her and apologized.

"It's all right, Kayla," she said. "I know this hasn't been easy for you. I was only trying to help. I'm still your friend and I'll be here if you need to yell at me again."

Tears filled my eyes when she said that. It made me realize how much my friends meant to me. What would I do without them? I vowed to appreciate them more and not to lose my temper at one of them again.

I was at a party Kelly had at her grandparents' home when I ran into Tim, an older brother of one of my friends. Kelly's parents had moved to Virginia, but she wanted to finish her senior year with her friends in Davenport, so she was living with her grandparents.

I had known Tim for a long time. We started talking about the Senior Prom, scheduled for May 10th. Jamie had a date and looked forward to going. I was envious and at the same time angry. The baby had changed so much between Stephen and me. A long time ago, Stephen had said he would come home for prom or graduation—at least for one of these special events. Now I hadn't heard from him in so long, I knew he wouldn't keep his promise.

Tim looked at me. "Kayla, are you going to the Senior Prom?"

"I doubt it," I responded. It made me sad to think about it. I wanted to go, but it seemed unlikely now.

"Well, do you want to go?" he asked.

I was surprised by his question. I didn't think he was seriously asking me for a date, so I said, "Sure."

"Well, then let's go. I'll take you."

At that point, I could tell he meant it. Even though I was pregnant, he was going to take me to the prom! My heart felt light. Tim was nice and I was comfortable with him. It wouldn't be like going to prom with Stephen, but that was all right. At least I wouldn't miss the dance.

When I told Mom, she was surprised, and pleased.

"We'll have to do something special for a dress, Kayla," she said. "I know a woman who's a good seamstress. She could make something that will hide your stomach."

That sounded good to me. I felt like doing a pirouette—like when I was younger and practiced on the plywood platform on the apartment-stairway landing. I didn't know what the word pregnant meant then! Tim's invitation was amazing to me now. I hadn't told anyone I wanted to go to prom, but everything was working out just great. I would have loved to call Stephen and say, "See? I don't need you, Unsat! I'll go without you!"

The evening of the dance, I wore the prettiest white satin dress with spaghetti straps that bared my shoulders. It had a large ruffle below the waistline that disguised my pregnancy perfectly without looking like a disguise. I felt so elegant in it—even though I felt like an elephant. I had gained only 10 pounds and had never been this heavy in my life!

Tim drove my mother's car and we double-dated with his sister. We went to The Dock, but I was paying more than half of the expenses because Tim didn't have a job.

The Dock is a fairly expensive restaurant overlooking the Mississippi River. We were shown to our table by an attractive brunette with long, permed hair. Early diners were already seated, drinking wine or cocktails, and enjoying gourmet meals.

I loved this kind of restaurant. Ray and Mom had taken us to elegant dining establishments for years. I knew how to behave, what silverware to use and when to switch from one fork to another. More than once,

Mom had served a whole salmon at a party. It made me feel special and sophisticated to be dressed up and at The Dock. My mouth watered for lobster or sole almondine.

"What are you going to get?" I asked my date.

"A hamburger," he said.

I looked at him, thinking he was joking. When I realized he wasn't, I felt a hot flush of embarrassment creep up my face.

The waitress came and Tim ordered hamburgers for himself and me. She politely explained they didn't have hamburgers on the menu. Disgruntled, he argued with her, finally giving in and ordering something else.

All evening long, it went like that. I barely talked to Tim. There didn't seem to be a whole lot to say. He didn't want to dance and later, he was so tired from being out late the night before that he slept through the post-party. Jamie and I sat together and tried to talk, but I was bored. I thought it would be such a great evening, and it wasn't. I enjoyed being at the dance, so I guess that's what counted most. The decorations were festive and exciting. At least I could say I hadn't missed out on the Senior Prom because of my pregnancy.

Stephen seemed to have forgotten ever knowing me. Mrs. Brown, my counselor at T.A.P.P, told me a lot of young fathers are like that. They say they love you, but when a pregnancy occurs and they're put to the test, they seem to disappear from the face of the earth, leaving the girls to fend for themselves.

One spring day, when the weather was warm and inviting, Heather and I decided to play "hookey" from school. We were both tired of being pregnant and sick of going to classes. We just wanted to get away from everything. We went to my house to get some bread because it was closer to school for feeding the ducks and swans at VanderVeer Park.

Heather's stomach was much bigger although we were due to deliver our babies about the same time. She would deliver only a week or so before me.

At the park, after Heather tied her brown hair back into a pony tail, we took off our shoes. With difficulty, we sat down on the edge of the water and felt the calm, warm breeze on our bare feet. A pair of mallards hovered near some children who were tossing chunks of bread into the water. Now, I handed Heather a crust; she broke it and began tossing bits onto the pond, where they were quickly gobbled up by a pair of mallards.

The swans rested on the water, gliding with folded wings along their sides. They turned their heads this way and that to study us. Heather laughed at them until she spied the cygnets, or young swans.

"Oh, look, Kayla! Babies!" she cried. "Aren't they something?"

I agreed. They were light-fawn colored and covered with a layer of soft down. They were bigger than one hand, but still small enough to fit into two hands cupped together. We fed the four until one turned its body toward us.

"Oh, look, Heather! It has a fishhook in its breast. The poor thing."

We watched as the cygnet nipped at the string attached to the fish hook. The cruelty of it tore at my heart. I cringed, feeling the imaginary pain of the metal piercing my skin.

"It keeps trying to bite it out," she said. "Oh, it must hurt. Why would anyone do that to a baby? Why doesn't someone help it?"

We didn't know what to do. We went to the nearby conservatory and looked until we found someone to help us. A man told us to call the Davenport Parks and Recreation Department. The girl who answered the 'phone said they were aware of the problem and had called the owner to take care of the baby swan.

Feeling better, we returned to the lake and feeding the ducks and swans. The sun felt good and I enjoyed being with Heather. She was a calm sort of person who had long ago decided she would keep her baby and continue to live with her family. She, too, had been deserted by her boyfriend, the son of a wealthy executive in a nearby town. As soon as his parents found out Heather was pregnant, they made him leave the service so he couldn't have his pay garnisheed for child support, and sent him to live on the West Coast. Although Heather's parents were good people—her father had been a major in the military and her mother is a nurse—the father's parents didn't feel Heather was a socially acceptable wife for their son. Not long afterward, Heather learned the father of her child had married a wealthy girl. His life was full, but her baby was fatherless. It had been a tough year for Heather, too.

As we sat there, I heard a motorcyle and immediately thought of Stephen. When I turned in the direction of the noise, I was astonished to see it *was* him! I couldn't believe it.

On the back of his bike, he had a girl, her blonde hair blowing from the motorcycle's speed. Stephen turned back to yell something into the wind. They both laughed.

"Heather, it's Stephen," I said, as she turned in his direction. "He's with a girl."

A huge knot of jealousy and anger swept through me. I didn't want to care, but I couldn't help myself. Once I had been on the back of that motorcycle. Once it had been me with my arms tight around his waist, my body pressing into his back. I could smell his freshly washed shirt, and his aftershave.

Tears smarted my eyes but I acted like it was no big deal. I forgot all about the ducks and the beautiful spring day. Heather reached over and placed her cool hand on my arm. It was obvious she didn't know what to say.

"How could he do this to me?" I whispered hoarsely. "I'm pregnant with his baby and he's out having a good time. How could he forget about me . . . and the baby?" I sobbed as Heather put her arm around me and laid my face on her shoulder.

"I know, Kayla," she said. "Believe me, I know." She started to cry with me.

"I just don't understand how he could do that, Heather." I sobbed.

Together, we cried into each other's arms. We sobbed to the ducks, the swans, the trees and the pond at VanderVeer Park.

8

Keeping Secrets

It was May 31st and Mom and my friends convinced me I should graduate with my class at Assumption High. At first, I didn't want to. I thought everyone would stare at me. But since I hadn't turned into a huge balloon, and remembering I would wear a robe, I began to think about it more. After all, I hadn't been so uncomfortable at the spaghetti dinner or at prom. And I wanted to graduate with my friends and classmates. Also, there was a Breakfast Mass honoring seniors and I didn't want to miss it. Mom decided to have another special dress made for the day's events.

On graduation day, I was out picking up clothes from the dry cleaners. When I arrived home, Mom was flying around the house in a panic—like a chicken with her head cut off. She was picking up dishes and leftovers from the evening meal like crazy, hiding everything in the dishwasher or refrigerator—whichever was appropriate.

I'd never seen her so flustered. "What's with Mom?" I asked Aaron.

"Grandma's coming for your graduation," he answered matter-of-factly, like nothing was wrong. "Aunt Glenda's going to be here, too."

My head started to reel. It hit me all at once, like I had been bombarded with it. I thought I would faint.

By the time I was six months pregnant, we still hadn't told any relatives—with the exception of my father—that I was pregnant.

We had our reasons . . . lots of them. Only recently, Grandma Becker had gone through the same situation with a cousin of mine, Teresa, who was deaf and had gotten pregnant. Teresa kept her child and Grandma felt Aunt Glenda had been saddled with most of the responsibility. My cousin could never hear the baby crying so it was up to her mother to help out. We didn't have the heart to tell Grandmother I was pregnant, too.

I knew I was going to give my baby up for adoption; we wanted to save all of my aunts and uncles the grief of knowing. I suppose we didn't want to feel any embarrassment or shame with them, either. I really felt bad about not telling our relatives—about hiding this from Grandmother—but we didn't want to hurt anyone more than we had to. My immediate family had suffered enough trauma to make up for all of the grandparents, aunts, uncles and cousins! After all, it seemed the kinder thing to do.

We had invited everyone to graduation, but it was a fair distance to drive, and we didn't expect anyone to come. It was really a surprise that Grandma Becker and Aunt Glenda had come to town for it unannounced.

Mom, flying through the dining room with a dust cloth, said they would be at the school and we were to meet them there. From the way Mom was cleaning, I could tell she thought they might come to the house afterwards.

As I mingled with my classmates and teachers at the senior breakfast, everyone came up to me and asked how I was getting along. There was one other pregnant classmate there and she was really big. Several students told me they couldn't tell I was expecting a baby. The new dress and the robe disguised my sixth-month condition better than the clown suit or my prom dress had.

When we arrived at the school, we looked for my grandmother and aunt but we couldn't find them. Because we were invited to Jamie's house for a party afterwards, Mom had told them to meet us there. I breathed a sigh of relief. At least for now, I was safe from discovery.

All during ceremonies, I felt so glad to be on the stage with my class. Students are always glad to celebrate graduation from high school, but I think I appreciated it more than anyone.

We had 129 students in our senior class. Bishop O'Keefe was there and former Senator Roger Jepsen (Democrat, Iowa) gave a speech. Afterwards, there were lots of parties and offers of drinks. I wouldn't drink anything alcoholic—it could hurt my baby, so I sat there and talked to people.

Grandma Becker's greeting is one I'll never forget!

"Don't I get a hug from the graduate?" she asked when she first saw me. "You look so pretty today, Kayla."

Panic gripped me. I didn't want to hug *anyone* in my condition. I looked at Mom but she didn't say anything. Her eyes were sending signals, but I couldn't read them. What should I do? I couldn't refuse. I took a deep breath and stepped forward, hoping she didn't notice my hesitation.

I put my arms around her and only allowed the upper part of our bodies to touch.

"It's good to see you, Grandma Becker," I said fondly. "Thanks for coming."

"I wouldn't miss it for the world. My son Michael's only daughter? You couldn't keep me away!"

She seemed to be satisfied and I breathed another sigh of relief. The crisis seemed to have passed. She hadn't noticed a thing!

After a short visit, she and my aunt left, and I breathed a sigh of relief. I could tell Mom felt more calm. She didn't act so flustered!

The next day, I had a private graduation party at the summerhouse with Jamie, Eileen, Madge, Kelly and Jamie's cousin. Ray had bought the land on the Mississippi River long before we knew him and built the house a little at a time, later adding a pool. We were there right after breakfast and stayed for almost five hours. I watched Jamie, Madge, and Eileen go down the slide at the same time. Laughing, they put an inner tube around my stomach to protect my baby when I was in the pool. The sun was hot and we sunburned, but I thought it was worth it.

The month of May turned out to be a good one. I felt so lucky to be included in prom and graduation ceremonies. I was so grateful to my friends. They didn't desert me—even when I had no patience or couldn't share some of their everyday concerns.

It was as if I had grown up overnight. The things I used to worry about—teachers, tests and boyfriends—were important to me once. But no longer.

I was seventeen and pregnant. But the worst was yet to come.

9

No Big Deal

By the first part of July, I was pretty much quarantined to the house. I felt like I had leprosy.

I was eight months pregnant and I was showing even though I hadn't ballooned as much as Heather or some of the other girls at T.A.P.P. It made me uncomfortable to have people looking at me, so I stayed home, isolating myself from the rest of the world.

Lately, I had begun to itch all over like crazy. My arms, my legs, my stomach—it was so bad I couldn't sleep at night. Nothing seemed to help. Not only was I big and clumsy, but I wanted to scratch constantly. I knew I was hard to live with. If I went with my friends to parties and movies, I was so uncomfortable sitting for any period of time that I was miserable. All I wanted to do was stay home. I really felt terrible about myself.

On the Fourth of July, Mom's sister and her brother and their families came for a week's stay at the summerhouse on the Mississippi River. Mom and I talked about whether to tell them about my pregnancy and together we decided not to. I didn't want to face them, so Mom said I was out of town when I really wasn't. It was hard for her to tell a lie and sad for me because I really wanted to see them.

While my family and relatives partied poolside, I ate by myself in the house on Marquette Street. I was lonely, so I steeped like a teabag in a cup, drowning in feelings of self-pity. I felt more and more like I was being punished. It seemed unfair, yet some of the time, I thought I deserved to suffer for the pain I had caused.

Once or twice while they were in the Quad-Cities, my relatives visited with my family at the Marquette Street house. I went to Eileen's until they left. When I drove by to see if I could come home yet, I saw the children playing in the front yard. It was like knowing about a party but being excluded from the guest list. It hurt.

Nevertheless, I survived the holiday weekend, and later that month, on Tuesday, July 16th, Mom and I started Natural Childbirth classes. I had dreaded them for months even though Heather and her mother were going at the same time. Heather and I arrived early at Davenport Medical Center, with a pillow under one arm and our mothers at our sides. I thought Heather was better equipped—her mother is a nurse!

Deep inside, I wished I could be experiencing this as a *real* couple; I resented the fact that the father of my child was hundreds of miles away.... I wondered if Heather felt the same way.

The class was conducted by a member of the Childbirth Education Association of the Mississippi Valley, Inc., and was held in the basement of the Davenport Medical Center in a large, barren room.[1] When we first started, we sat in a circle and there were first-name introductions.

1. Childbirth Education Association of the Mississippi Valley, Inc., is not hospital- or doctor-affiliated. I planned to deliver at St. Lukes' Hospital.

Linda Cloghessy, a childbirth educator, was our teacher. Her dark, curly hair almost touched her shoulders. Her green eyes sparkled over the spattering of freckles across her nose. She made a few opening remarks, telling us she was there to listen to our problems and help us through the labor and delivery. She would not offer any opinions or advice unless she was invited to do so.

When she introduced a group participation activity, my heart skipped a beat. I wanted to melt into the class, and now she was going to make everyone look at me and I would have to talk. I didn't have aspirations to be a public speaker in my condition!

"What I'd like to do now is go around the circle and have each one of you talk about what's good and what's bad about this pregnancy," she said, smiling with encouragement. She pointed to one mother and suggested we start with her.

There were about seven young women in the class. A few were with their husbands and one had brought her boyfriend. Most of us were accompanied by our mothers.

Each one spoke in turn, reciting positive results from her pregnancy experience. Several said they were looking forward to the baby being born. It was like they were talking about buying a new toy. Everyone shared the names they had picked and talked about all of the fun things you can do with a baby. No one mentioned the hard work—early morning feedings, illnesses or messy pants.

Then it was Mom's turn. She looked so serious; her voice was calm and smooth. She was wearing her favorite perfume and for once Giorgio didn't make me nauseous.

"Well, I can't see a lot of positive things about this pregnancy," she said, looking around to other members of the circle. "First of all, Kayla had to drop out of school. She was very sick, and it caused a lot of turmoil in our family. The only positive thing I can see is that we're a lot closer now and it brought us to realize some feelings we hadn't expressed in a long time."

She cleared her throat and went on. She had tears in her eyes and her voice was thick with emotion. She played with the fabric of her skirt and her diamond glistened in the light.

"I can't see a lot of positive things about learning your teenaged daughter is pregnant—knowing everything that's ahead of her in the next few months. It's been very hard for all of us to deal with this."

The room was filled with silence as she finished. I was next.

I burned with embarrassment when all eyes turned to me. I took a deep breath and began to speak. I didn't want to look at anyone. So I glanced at Heather and she smiled encouragement.

"I'm going to give my baby up for adoption. We've found a really nice home for him—or her," I added, smiling. "The parents are good ones—they're young and they're of the same faith I am, and I wanted that. The mother is a pre-school teacher who will stay home with the baby, and the father works for a corporation."

I finished speaking and looked at Mom. She smiled at me and I recognized that expression. It was one of pride. I'd seen it before—when I had danced well in a ballet recital, or had come home with good grades. She was proud of my answer. The first class ended on a good feeling.

Overall, I decided the classes were interesting and helpful. For example, one of my concerns was that I would be able to see and to care for my baby in the hospital. I wanted to have fond memories of my baby's first days of life. Linda, our instructor, suggested we clear it with hospital officials before I was admitted. Mom made several telephone calls on my behalf. She wanted to be assured that I wouldn't be discriminated against because I was a single mother.

Toward the end of the series of four classes, Linda told us her group didn't believe in withholding information about the birthing process. It was her way of introducing several films. They were what I would call "major graphic." They showed everything there was to see about having a baby . . . including a doctor performing an episiotomy. Even in the subdued lighting, I could feel my face burn with embarrassment.

One film in particular made Mom sick and I laughed at that. She'd had three kids! Why should she be affected by all of this? Later she laughed, too, and said her perspective was different as a spectator.

Even though I enjoyed these light-hearted moments, when I was a-lone, I was afraid. I remembered the films and all I could think was, "Oh, God, this just makes me more scared." And then over and over, "I don't want to go through this *at all*."

The next month dragged by day after day. August 9, my due date, came and went. Heather had her baby on the 14th and the following day I visited her in the hospital. I smiled and greeted her. The first thing she said was, "Oh, Kayla, you're going to die. It's worse than the films."

I swallowed hard, looked away, and didn't say anything. My chest felt as if it would burst and my hands were clammy cold. But then the nurse brought Heather's baby into the room. I held Sara Emilie, and looked into her little blue eyes. She was the sweetest baby even though she didn't have much hair. I wondered again what my baby would look like. I had been asking myself these questions for a long time.

Now, the answers were only a few days away.

I'd enrolled in classes at Scott Community College, but they started on the 19th and I didn't want to go while I was still pregnant. I called in sick and stayed home. To keep me busy, Mom put me to work addressing invitations to the grand opening of her business. On Thursday, August 22, after nearly two years of hard work and planning, she opened her designer clothing store. She was worried about what she'd do when I went into labor. How could she be in two places where she felt needed at the same time?

To complicate matters, Mom was scheduled to go on a buying trip to Dallas, Texas. When Linda Cloghessy announced in class she would make herself available to anyone wanting her support during labor and delivery, it seemed like the answer to our problem. We asked her to be there with me if Mom couldn't. As it turned out, Mom left and returned, and still nothing had happened.

On Monday when I went to the doctor, I still wasn't worried. I knew I was overdue, but it was no big deal. I was just sitting around, waiting for my water to break.

I didn't look forward to my visits with Dr. Izetti. He hadn't pressured me anymore about giving him the rights to conduct a private adoption, and I certainly didn't bring up the subject! We had formed a professional doctor-patient relationship, nothing more and nothing less. At one point, I almost switched doctors, but I decided to stick it out. I tolerated his abrupt bedside manner and looked forward to the day when all of this was over.

Dr. Izetti took me by surprise when he gave me an unexpected command. After he had examined me, he said calmly, "Well, come in tomorrow and I'll induce you."

I was shocked! I wasn't ready for that. I felt like I was falling out of control from a cliff, plummeting to the ground. I felt light-headed. Tomorrow was a definite appointment—I had liked not knowing when it would happen much better.

I told Mom and called Linda, my Lamaze teacher, who had offered to be with us at the delivery. Even though Mom would be there, I decided I wanted Linda there, too. She promised to meet us at the hospital.

The next morning, I went to St. Luke's Hospital, was admitted to a room, and put on the hospital gown. I was afraid. I didn't like hospitals and I didn't want to be a patient in one. I wanted a natural childbirth. I had been trained for it. Now, everything was happening too fast. I was so glad Mom and Linda were with me.

The nurses prepped me and Dr. Izetti broke my water. Nothing else seemed to happen. He told me I was having short contractions—they showed on the monitor. I couldn't feel a thing. The doctor said I was dilated about three centimeters.

Then they gave me an enema and I hated that. Still, nothing happened. A nurse administered an IV. I didn't like needles at all and they stuck me four times before they found the vein. The IV wasn't even working! At first they put small amounts of pitocin into the IV to make the contractions harder. When that didn't work, they added more.

I didn't want to have an IV, I didn't want to have anything. I had planned to deliver my baby without complications: no IV, no enema, no episiotomy. This was worse than the films!

By seven o'clock that night—nine hours later—I was still only dilated three centimeters. As the pitocin began to take effect, the contractions came harder and harder. The nurse gave me a pain shot and it made me sleepy. Even during the contractions, I was falling asleep. Linda and Mom kept saying, "Kayla, keep your eyes open." Mom touched my shoulder to reassure me of her presence.

In between contractions, Mom made several quick telephone calls, checking on the business. She talked with Connie (our housekeeper and long-time friend) outside the door, and Kirk Langer, who waited with Ray in the reception room. Mom rubbed my back, hugged me and planted an occasional kiss on my forehead. Only Mom and Linda, a childbirth educator, were allowed in the delivery room.

Despite everything that was going on around me, I couldn't forget my appearance. One time, as I squeezed Linda's hand, I felt her trying to cool my burning face with a washcloth. "No, don't," I said. "You'll mess up my makeup."

Every once in a while, when the nurse was out of eyesight, Connie Langer would crack the door just enough so she could hear. At one point, Kirk and Connie were allowed in the room briefly so they could pray for me and the safe delivery of my child. I can still hear the words in Kirk's deep, masculine voice: *Dear Lord, give Kayla the physical, emotional and spiritual strength to bring the child into the world and to make the difficult decision she faces. Let the child be healthy and blessed by your spirit . . . .*

Finally, about eight-thirty, I dilated to four, then to five centimeters, and everything started happening very fast. By 9:30, the doctor was there and I had my legs up in stirrups. And I said to myself, "Oh, God, this is it." I was so scared. It really hurt. When I looked at Mom, I could tell she was uncomfortable. Her expression was one of pained tolerance. After one hard contraction subsided, I said out loud, "Never again. I'm never gonna have kids. No way."

Mom and Linda laughed, piercing the veil of tension.

At 10:14 P.M. after 12 hours of labor, Keera was born. The doctor announced immediately that my baby was a girl. The news made me happy, but the emotion was overwhelming. My heart felt so full with happiness and at the same time a terrible sorrow—I couldn't prevent my tears. I had really wanted a girl and all along, I'd thought it was a girl.

I breathed a sigh of relief. The excitement buoyed my strength and I didn't want to close my eyes anymore! Connie Langer was outside the door again and had heard the doctor as he announced my daughter's delivery. She ran back and told Ray and Kirk.

A few minutes later, after the baby had been cleaned off, I held my daughter for the first time.

"It's a girl," Mom repeated, her voice filled with wonder. "Eight pounds, two and one half ounces. She's so beautiful." She began to cry.

My teacher, Linda, was still in the room. She told me what a good job I had done and she began crying. Even the nurse had glistening eyes.

When I held my baby for the first time, her eyes were scrunched, and she was crying up a storm. Her face was kind of chubby and she was all pink. They told me she was healthy; there were no problems. She had a lot of dark hair—more than usual for a newborn, Mom and Linda agreed.

When Ray came into the room and held Keera for the first time, he said, "Look how alert she is! She recognizes my voice."

"She looks like you, Kayla. She's just like you when you were a tiny baby," Mom said. Her eyes were still sad, reddened from her tears . . . , and filled with love for her first grandchild.

"Hello, Keera," I whispered to the warm, wonderful baby once she was back in my arms. "How are you feeling, Baby?"

I felt so strange! I couldn't stop crying, and I couldn't believe this little creature had come from my body. My stomach was all flat and I just couldn't believe it. I kept thinking, this is my baby. It was really cool. I began to feel it was all worth it.

Soon after delivery, I called Eileen, Madge and Jamie. Jamie was out of her dorm room, so I called Mrs. Livermore and she called Jamie later.

I was so hungry, a nurse went downstairs for a chocolate shake and a ham and swiss cheese sandwich. It tasted so good! I hadn't had anything to eat all day and during labor I couldn't keep down the apple juice they gave me.

Other visitors started coming the next day. Of course, Eileen, Madge, and Heather came. And so did Melissa. Cynthia, Mom's business manager, and Aaron and Ray also visited. The next day, Corey went to a funeral with some classmates and stopped on his way home.

The nurses brought Keera into me for each feeding because I had said I wanted to do it. I held her and loved her, feeling her delicate skin and smelling her baby fragrance. I took pictures of her and asked others to take pictures of me holding her. I treasured the moments, filled with the newfound wonder of a mother's love.

I had been told I shouldn't hold Keera or see her because it would make everything harder when it came time to let her go. But I thought I should spend as much time as possible with her. I wanted to have memories. I would have felt empty if I hadn't done it. Now, I'm glad because I know what it feels like to hold her close.

Keera usually stayed with me at least an hour before I took her back to the nursery or someone came to get her. It wasn't until the next day that I was up and walking around, but I was really sore and I had to walk like a bowlegged cowboy.

All the nurses on the maternity floor knew I was going to give her up for adoption. Sometimes one of them would come in and I'd be crying. One nurse kept saying, "It's going to be okay." I smiled through my tears, appreciating the kindness.

But it didn't help.

I was filled with doubts. I couldn't imagine what the adoptive couple were like. They sounded like nice people, but what did they look like? Were they really kind and loving? Would they take good care of my baby? Had I made a good choice?

I felt so confused. I knew the best thing for Keera was to give her up for adoption. But I wanted to keep her. I cried until the aching in my eyes matched that of my heart. And then I cried some more.

Time after time, I thanked God that my baby was so perfect, healthy and beautiful. My moods went from complete happiness in gratitude for these blessings to an awful depression when I thought about giving her up. She could be lost to me forever.

Mom knew I was having a hard time with my decision. She came into my room, sat on the bed next to me and put her soft, pretty hand over mine. She was wearing a new shade of nail polish.

Her brown eyes were sad. She acted discouraged. Her frosted, stylish brown hair framed a face that was full of pain and I knew it mirrored my own. People said we looked alike. Now, because I had passed the milestone between being a teenager and an adult, we probably looked more alike than ever.

"Kayla, you've been crying again, haven't you?" she asked. "Oh, Honey, I know how hard this is for you. But you have to think of what's best for Keera."

I nodded. The burden of my decision was more responsibility than I had imagined. Early on in the pregnancy, when the baby didn't seem so real to me, it sounded almost easy. Now I had touched her, held her and had formed an attachment to my baby that I didn't want to sever.

The whole world seemed bleak and dark. I didn't think the sun would ever come out for me again. There was no laughter in my life. I had no thoughts of riding on a motorcyle with my hair streaming in the wind. Or of parties with friends. What little joy I felt was fleeting—disappearing every time my tiny, beautiful daughter was returned to the nursery.

"Do you think it would help if you spoke with the adoptive mother?" Mom asked.

I hadn't thought of that. "I think so," I said.

She called the lawyer, told him how much I was vacillating in my decision, and asked if I could talk to the adoptive mother.

When Jacqueline (not her real name) called the next morning, we talked for about twenty minutes. At first, the conversation was awkward, but then, she took the lead. Her voice had a soft, soothing effect as she reassured me of their commitment to Keera.

"We'll really love that little girl," she said. "You know we don't have other children, so your baby will receive our undivided attention." She laughed softly. "We'll probably spoil her rotten if you'll let us."

Jacqueline was picking her words carefully; I could hear the emotion in her voice. She was fighting, in her own way, to help me stay with my original decision. I knew how badly they wanted my child.

"Kayla, we really appreciate what you're doing for her and for us," she said. "It takes someone very brave to do this—to let your child go. I know how hard it must be for you. But we really want this baby. We'll take good care of her always."

But I wanted Keera, too. Right now, I wanted her more than college, more than parties and boyfriends, more than anything I had ever known in my life. I had carried her, loved her, fed and changed her. She was mine.

Oh God, why did it have to hurt so much?

"Did you know I was adopted, too?" Jacqueline said, finally. "I never found my birth parents, but I've always wondered about them. If you ever want your baby to know about you, I'll tell her at an early age she was adopted."

Tears ran down my cheeks. I couldn't keep the sobbing from my voice. I clutched the telephone receiver like a lifeline.

"I just don't want the baby—when she gets older—to think I didn't love her because I'm doing this."

"It's okay, Kayla," she said. "She'll know how much you love her. She'll know why it's the best thing . . . why we're raising her instead of you."

Jacqueline told me the name they had picked for the baby. Her choice of a middle name, coincidentally, was Marie. It was the same as mine. I told her I thought that was nice and she agreed.

After we said good-bye, I continued to cry, but I felt better. The call had helped me. I didn't hurt any less, but once again I thought I could do it.

Jamie was in school at the University of Northern Iowa and couldn't visit me until later in the week—just before Labor Day Weekend. She came directly to the hospital, and hadn't taken time to unpack. She brought me a miniature dog sculpture as a gift. I opened it carefully. It's blue eyes were realistic, but they weren't warm and alive like Keera's.

I was dressed in the white maternity slacks and red blouse I had worn the day I was admitted. Jamie stayed with me all afternoon, sitting in the chair or on the side of my bed. We watched television and talked most of the time. She told me about the boys she was dating, her classes and the teachers she liked and disliked.

"There's this really cute boy. I've been trying to get his attention," Jamie said dreamily. "He's in my English comp class, but he always sits on the other side of the room."

I tried to be polite, yet I wasn't much interested in hearing about new boyfriends. My mind kept wandering to thoughts of Keera.

"Kayla, why don't you come to the University of Northern Iowa?" she asked. "We could share a dorm room. It would be great."

"Yeah, maybe," I answered. "I really don't want to think about that now."

Even though Jamie was with me, I couldn't stop thinking about Keera. Her tiny face was so vivid in my thoughts. I could feel her little body, imagine my lips on her cheek and smell her. My nostrils were filled with the sweet, unique smell of my baby. My fingers could feel the fine, silky hair. She was such a miracle.

As the tears started again, Jamie looked at me and I could tell she felt bad. She looked quiet, withdrawn and worried.

"Kayla, please stop, or I'm going to start crying too," she threatened softly. She gave me a big hug and started crying. "Don't worry," she said. "I love you and I'll always be your friend."

We sat there and cried together. I didn't try to talk. I couldn't. All I could think about was this terrible ache in my chest.

"Go ahead and cry, Kayla," Jamie said, blowing her nose hard on a tissue. "It'll make you feel better."

I smiled at her. It made me feel good to know that she cared so much.

After a while, Jamie and I went to the nursery and picked up Keera. She was wrapped in white—a tiny, warm bundle of love and innocence. Jamie accepted a bottle from the nurse and we brought Keera back to my room. I held her and fed her, watching the little mouth and cheeks working furiously. Her blue eyes looked at me the whole time.

"Hi, Keera," I said softly. "You're looking well today. You're my baby, aren't you? You'll always be my baby."

I knew she recognized my voice. I began to cry.

I looked up when I heard a familiar clicking of heels on the tile floor. Mom had said she'd be here to pick me up at one o'clock. But she was so busy with the new store, she couldn't get away until four P.M. Perhaps she had been putting off the final parting, dreading it as much as I was.

Mom entered the room and nodded, with a sad smile, at Jamie. As Mom and Jamie watched me, tears streamed down their cheeks. A nurse brought in a wheelchair.

"Come on, Kayla," Mom said, sobbing, "we have to go."

I held Keera for the last time, kissed her good-bye, and touched my finger to her satiny cheek before putting her back in the bassinette. My tears spotted the white blanket as I drank in the sight of her, my heart aching. Mom put her arm around me and pulled me to her. I buried my face in her shoulder and my tears soiled her elegant dress. She put her cheek on my head and cried.

"It's time, Kayla," she said. "We have to go sometime."

I nodded.

Mom and Jamie collected my suitcase and my gifts and we left Keera there with the nurse.

I'd only held her a dozen times, but now my arms felt so empty.

The three of us walked down the hall, Mom's heels clicking loudly. No one spoke. All I could think about was that tiny face, those blue, blue eyes.

The pregnancy was over, and with it, nine months of my life were behind me. I had walked away. It hurt, but I had done it. All I had to show for my experience were some cards, pink and yellow carnations, and a miniature sculptured puppy with realistic eyes.

Tomorrow morning, the attorney was coming with the relinquishment papers.

I knew I couldn't sign them.

10

Time Runs Out

When I arrived home, I felt like I had been gone long enough for an extended vacation, although I'd only been gone three days. We had withheld our permission for an announcement in the newspaper. Close friends and family knew I'd had my baby.

Nothing had changed, I thought. Except me. I'm changed forever.

Once inside the house, Mom went one way, and Jamie and I went another. In my blue and white bedroom, I closed the door, walked to my bed and sank face down on it. Jamie sat on the edge next to me, gently placing her hand on my shoulder. Before long, my pillow sham was soaked with tears. Would they never stop, I wondered? Will I cry over this baby for the rest of my life?

Jamie didn't try to talk to me. We were the closest kind of friends.... two people who find quiet companionship and are comfortable with each other. She didn't have to make idle conversation and I was glad she didn't.

When my sobs stilled for the hundredth time in the last few days, I rolled over, wiped my eyes with the back of my hand, and looked at her. Her eyes were full of sadness. They, too, were wet and red from her tears. I pulled a tissue from my pocket and wiped my nose.

Snotty nose, I thought. Someone else will be wiping Keera's runny nose.

"Hey, Kayla, let's go out tomorrow," Jamie said, brightening. "We'll go to a restaurant for breakfast and then walk around the mall. It'll be fun."

"No, I'm too exhausted. I haven't been eating much lately, either. Besides, I have to stay home until nine o'clock. The attorney is coming with the papers."

I dreaded seeing him again. The thought of signing away my baby was more than I could bear. I just didn't think I could do it.

"I have a headache, Jamie," I said, placing my hand on my forehead. "Will you bring me two aspirin from the bathroom drawer? Please?"

"Well, what about after he leaves?" she asked, as she went for the aspirin. Her voice drifted back from the bathroom. "You should try to get your mind off this. It would do you some good."

"I suppose," I said dully. "But it's a lie."

"What's a lie?" Jamie said, returning with the aspirin and a glass of water. She handed me the tablets and the glass. I swallowed them like they were vitamins and drank every drop, then handed the glass back to her. My throat was hot and parched. My eyes burned. I wanted to hold my face under a cold shower and let it cleanse my skin. I wished it could wash away my troubles and the aching in my soul. But no amount of water could do that and even I knew it.

"What the nurse said . . . what Dad said . . . that it'll be okay," I said quietly. "I don't think it'll ever be okay again."

Jamie stared at me, momentarily stopped in her tracks.

Before she left, we made arrangements that I would call her if I wanted to go out. Alone again, I showered and climbed into pajamas even though it was only five-thirty in the afternoon. I didn't feel like socializing with my family at a meal and besides, I wasn't hungry. I crawled between the cool sheets and tried to sleep.

But I couldn't.

Later, when Mom brought me some fruit, milk and a sandwich, I nibbled at the food, but I couldn't enjoy a bite. She tried to talk to me and I didn't encourage her. I think she understood how awful I felt and wanted to ease me through all this with as little pain as possible. But we both knew it was too late for that. It would be a long time before anything could return to normal. She left, and with her leaving, her soft, soothing voice and gentle manner were gone too. Suddenly, my room felt like a tomb and I was lonely.

I wondered what Keera's father was doing at that very minute. Was he in a chowline somewhere, or eating a meal in a ditch while on maneuvers? I hadn't heard from him since March. *Why hadn't he written in so long?* I hoped he was suffering some regrets, but I wouldn't take any bets on it.

I slept fitfully that night. I kept waking and seeing Keera's tiny face. I rolled over to see the time; it was exactly two o'clock—her feeding time. I pictured a nurse in a white uniform, smiling at Keera and talking softly while she fed my baby. I missed my daughter. I missed holding her and feeding her and talking to her.

Fresh tears flowed with this new wave of grief. Pain was like the sea—it continued to splash on the shore, pausing only for brief reprieves. Sometimes the waves were smaller than others—but more often than not—they engulfed me.

"Why, God?" I asked the dark night. "Why did this have to happen to me? Why didn't I prevent it? Why doesn't Stephen love me any more? Why doesn't he care what his daughter looks like? Why? Why? Why?"

I had a million questions that had no answers. I hated Stephen for not writing in so long. I'd given up on hearing from him again. In all fairness, I realized he didn't know about his daughter. But at least part of that was his fault.

As I lay awake, thinking, the minutes on the clock flew by. I couldn't help but wonder if I'd ever have peaceful rest again. Now, and then, I dozed fitfully.

The next morning, Mom roused me and reminded me to be ready for the attorney's meeting. My body ached. I was still sore from my stitches and a bad night's rest hadn't done anything to help me.

I knew what I had to do. But I didn't want to sign those papers. I wanted to keep my daughter. I didn't want to let her go to these strangers who merely sounded pleasant over the telephone. At this moment, I didn't give a darn how great or financially able they were. Keera was mine and no one could ever love her or want her more than I did.

When the attorney and the two women came to the door, Mom let them in and called to me in my room, "Kayla, they're here." Slowly, I came out and Mr. Nash introduced his wife, and Mrs. Nelson, a friend of the adoptive couple. He explained it's a state law that there be two witnesses present.

We went first to the living room, before Mom suggested the use of the dining table might be more helpful when signing papers. We arranged ourselves and a meeting that lasted only an hour seemed to take forever. In my mind, no amount of torture could have been more painful. What could be worse than having your heart ripped from your body?

Yet I knew I had to sign for Keera's sake. She deserved to have two parents who had more time for her. There would be so many things I couldn't give Keera if I kept her. I didn't want to go on welfare to raise her. I remembered how much Mom had hated accepting charity. That had been a distinct possibility when I first became pregnant. It still was. I knew I couldn't live at home forever.

My head told me one thing and my heart begged for another solution to my problem.

As I struggled to find the courage to sign the papers in front of me, I could hear those around me crying. The attorney, his wife and the adoptive couple's friend—virtually all strangers—suffered with me. Mom and Ray had lived with agony for months. I knew it, but at this moment, I didn't care. None of them could hurt as much as I did. Maybe Mom, or Ray, but it wasn't the same. I was Keera's mother.

The first attempt to sign failed. I couldn't bring myself to do it. I couldn't see the line through my tears. I could barely get my breath between sobs.

Mom cleared her throat. "Kayla, if you're not ready to do this, we don't have to do it. It can be put off until another time."

"Well, Kathryn, we have to do something today," the lawyer interrupted, contradicting Mom. "The doctor has discharged the baby and she has to leave the hospital. If you don't sign today, then you'll have to make provisions for the baby to come here. You're not giving me permission to take this baby and place her."

"Kayla, honey, if you bring her home, you'll never let her go," Mom said. Her voice was soft and sad.

I sat there, staring at the pen, crying. My cold hands were clasped in front of me.

"Kayla, if you can't sign it . . . ," Mom's voice drifted off.

"No, I can sign it. I can sign it. I have to do it. I'm not going to change my mind. It's for the best. She needs to be in a better home than I can give her."

I wiped my eyes and again picked up the pen. I pushed all thoughts of Keera from my mind, braced myself, scribbled my name, *Kayla Marie Becker*, and released the pen. It clattered to the table. Then I threw my head down on my arms and wept—feeling utterly, hopelessly lost to my daughter and her to me.

After everyone was gone, I felt a hand on my shoulder, recognized my mother's touch and looked up. My throat was hot and dry again—a familiar feeling over the past few days.

"Oh, I wish I wouldn't have done it. I wish I wouldn't have done it."

"Kayla, I wish you had let them take her to Mrs. Nelson's home to give you a few more days to think about this decision."

I sat up and looked at my mother, sobbing. "I didn't want to do it! I didn't want to do it! I wish I wouldn't have done it!"

"Then you have only once choice, Kayla. You have to call the lawyer and tell him you changed your mind and the baby is to go to Mrs. Nelson's to give you a few more days."

I convinced Mom to call the hospital for me. She talked to the nurse on the maternity floor before the lawyer arrived. The nurse took a message and a few minutes later, he called back, talking to my mother before asking to speak with me. I was the mother; it was my decision.

I got on the phone, visualizing the attorney's frustration as I started to talk.

"I want her to go to the friends' home—Mrs. Nelson's. I need a little more time."

"Is this your decision?" he asked. "You, and only you are the one making this decision?"

"Yes," I said. "Oh yes, it's just me."

As I hung up the telephone, I sighed deeply. I felt as if a terrible burden had been lifted from my shoulders.

I picked up the 'phone again and automatically dialed Jamie's number. When she answered, for the first time in days I said something happily: "Are you ready for breakfast?"

"I'll be right over," she replied.

Jamie and I sat across the table from each other in the no-smoking section at the Village Inn. After we ordered juice and pancakes with cherry topping and whipped cream, I told her about the meeting with the attorney.

"It was worse than the delivery," I said. "But I did it. Mom didn't think I could do it, but I did. I made myself sign that piece of paper."

Jamie looked at me sympathetically. "So now what, Kayla?" she asked. "What will you do now?"

"I don't know," I said, "but I have 96 hours to reverse my decision and keep her." I looked at my pancakes and suddenly lost my appetite. "I miss her, Jamie. I miss her more than I thought I ever could. I don't want to give her up."

Jamie nodded. She didn't try to force her opinions on me. I knew she could accept whatever I chose to do. She knew how hard all of this had been on me and my family. Because of her friendship with me, she had suffered. It had been hard on her, too.

Our order came, with the check, and we ate.

Between bites, I told Jamie about my promise to Mom to attend college classes.

"And then I'll have to get a part-time job to help pay for books and a babysitter," I said.

"Boy, it would be really hard to do all of that," Jamie replied. I nodded. I thought so too. But I felt I knew what "hard" meant. Life had been increasingly difficult and complicated since last December when I learned I was pregnant.

We finished, picked up the bill and paid it at the counter. Back in the car, we drove the short distance to the mall where Jamie parked near the center-front entrance.

As we started to walk down center court, Jamie leaned over to me and said, "Have you ever seen so many babies in your life?"

I nodded. She wasn't the first to notice.

My heart ached for my own baby. I thought I was going to die. Everywhere we looked, there were mothers, fathers, young children and grandparents pushing a baby carriage or stroller.

As if in a nightmare, every one of the babies turned into the image of my daughter.

When we walked by Mothercare, a maternity shop with baby and toddler clothes, Jamie tried to distract me.

"It's okay, Jamie," I said. "I'll be okay."

We turned left, walking with the curve of the mall, then right at the shoe store, and on toward Younker's, a large department store. Along the way, Jamie stopped to look at clothes and tried to interest me in a new skirt, or a blouse. Usually I loved shopping. Now, nothing seemed worth caring about. Clothes had never seemed so insignificant to me.

Everywhere we went, Jamie tried to spare me any more pain. She tried to make me laugh and take my mind off my daughter. After a while, I told Jamie I was tired and asked to sit for a while. We stayed about an hour before going home.

For the next three days, I cried. I thought about Keera all the time. Mom and I talked about it over and over, arguing the same points, discussing the same problems and obstacles.

All day long, I was on an emotional roller coaster. My decision fluctuated back and forth, and with it my mood swings went from excitement and joy to depression and despair. I prayed for guidance and I prayed for support. I prayed for Keera.

I didn't sleep at all.

At four o'clock in the morning on the second day, I went in to talk to Mom.

"I don't think I can do it," I said. "I just keep seeing her little face all the time. She probably misses me because she knew my voice. She's probably wondering where I am. I'm going to keep her."

Mom sat up, her eyes were dark with circles and the lack of sleep. Even without makeup, I thought she was pretty. Her delicate bone structure and smooth skin were flattered by the pink gown she wore. Ray stirred and listened quietly while my mother and I talked.

"She's in a good home, Kayla. A few days won't make a big difference. She's so young right now. You need the time to think about this."

"I just don't want to do it, Mom, . . . give her up, I mean." I said my tears were like the rains around Noah's Ark. They never seemed to stop falling. "I want to keep her. I can do it. I know I can."

"You can do it if you want to, Honey. I know you can raise her. But remember that trip to Florida for a visit with your father? What would it be like with a baby along? Cancel that. Cancel all those fun, growing up things because you're going to be a full-time mother. If you can honestly say you'll give her all the attention a baby should have . . . that she'll be the focus of your life and that you won't have any regrets later on—blaming her for missing out on all the things your friends are doing—

"If you put her above everything else in your life, then keep her. Because that's what you need to do for a baby and that's what I did for all of you when you were babies," she said honestly. "But if you can't say that she's going to be number one, then you're not doing her any favors. You have to think of what's best for Keera. Not 'what I want,' not 'how much I love her,' not 'how much I miss her,' but what's really best for the next 20 years."

She paused. I didn't want to listen to a lecture, but deep in my heart, I knew she was right.

"You know yourself, not having had a father around all the time, that it's difficult. You don't know much about raising babies. But I know if you want to do it badly enough, you can learn.

"Kayla honey, I prayed about this. Tomorrow morning, we're going to face this, and whatever you decide, God will give us the strength to deal with it. I'll know it's His will. So if you can't let her go, then keep her and we'll make the best of it," she said. "But you have to promise me you'll go to school so your life won't pass you by. And that you won't be sitting home and taking care of the baby all the time. You have to go out and socialize."

"I promise."

I stood there, feeling better, but not ready to leave. I started thinking about how many hours I'd be away from the baby.

"Mom, I'll never see her. I'll only be with her in the afternoon," I said. "If I get a job and go to school parttime, I'll never see Keera." Biting my lip, I looked away.

Mom didn't say anything and neither did Ray.

Tears fell down my cheeks. "Well, I think I can do it. I can let her go," I said, switching for probably the 60th time. "I think it's the best thing for her to have a mother and a father and they're prepared for a baby and I'm not prepared at all. They're going to love her and they've been waiting a long time to have a baby.

"She's going to be loved, I know that," I said, tears rolling down my cheeks. "She's going to be in a good home. If I kept her, I'd only be thinking of myself, I wouldn't be thinking of her at all. I'd just be thinking of my love for her."

I thought about how it would be later in her life, trying to explain about her father, and what I'd have to tell her.

"If she has her adoptive parents, it won't matter that her father deserted her . . . that he didn't love her or want her. Maybe somehow she'll know how much I wanted her," I said, sobbing.

Ray didn't say a word, but followed my mother's lead and let me talk.

"I don't want her to think I didn't love her," I continued. "I don't want her growing up and being known as illegitimate. So I think I can do it."

Mom smiled at me and opened her arms. I went to her and let her hug me, feeling the warmth of being loved. I knew Mom and Ray would support any decision I made; they had said so. Once they told me I couldn't keep Keera and live at home with her, but they had reversed their statement. Now, they said they would support any decision I made and do their best to help me.

I said, "Well, if I kept the baby, I could go to school in the mornings and Keera would be with a babysitter until I got home. I wouldn't have any social life, but I don't think it really matters. The baby would be with me and everything would be fine."

"You have to make your decision by tomorrow, so we'll have time to buy baby things," Mom said. "You can't keep changing your mind forever; you have to make a final decision."

Mom was frustrated that I couldn't stick with my decision, but I think she understood my dilemma. As soon as I talked myself into keeping Keera, I became depressed because I knew a part-time job and school would leave me little time to spend with my daughter. My mood swings went from the top of the mountain because I had decided to keep her . . . to the bottom of the valley when I had reaffirmed my original decision to release her for adoption.

Even Mom's early discussions had taken on a new tone. I remembered one night before Keera had been born, Mom had said, "Well, are you going to give the baby up for adoption? I think you should."

Now, she and Ray had mixed feelings. They wanted me to keep her and they wanted me to let her go. They knew it would be really hard for me to raise her and still earn an education.

Sunday morning, Mom made me get up early. "Okay, Kayla, let's get ready. We going to go out and shop for baby things."

I rolled over to face her. "No, Mom, I made up my mind. I'm letting her go."

She looked at me, as if she didn't believe it was my final decision. She nodded, and left the room. All day long, there seemed to be a sense of morbid calm around about me. I felt like someone had died and I couldn't do anything about it. I spent most of the day in my room, watching television, reading, or thinking about my baby. I ached with an intense inner pain that refused to go away.

That night I went to bed and tossed and turned until the early hours of Monday morning.

Suddenly, Ray appeared at my door, saying, "Kayla, your mother needs to talk to you." I threw back the covers, put on slippers and a robe, and we went up the white, spiral staircase to the master bedroom.

"It's okay, Mom, I've decided."

"I know," she said, clearing her throat as her eyes filled with tears. "I'm feeling that I may have influenced you too much. Maybe I pushed you into this . . . I could have made it easier for you and supported you more through all of this."

"Mom, you're just making it harder for me. Every time you start crying, then I start crying and having doubts."

"I'm sorry, Kayla, but I have to know. You have to convince me that this is your decision and you're not going to be angry at me later on...."

"No, Mom, I'm not. You didn't push me into it. It's my decision and I think it's best for Keera."

"It's got to be your own decision. But you also have to raise her," she said. "I—I just don't want you to come back to me some day and say I forced you into all of this."

We talked for two hours before I kissed Mom on the cheek and went back to bed. I finally fell asleep about three o'clock and woke up with only three minutes remaining. I watched the clock tick away as if I were watching a rocket countdown: 5:13, 5:14 and finally 5:15.

Something should have happened. A bomb should have exploded, or a fire alarm should have gone off. But nothing happened. Time just ran out. My time to be a mother had come too soon. I wasn't ready. So I let my baby go.

Some say that such an act takes courage. Others call it a mother abandoning her child. I only know I did what I felt was best for the life of my daughter. She didn't deserve to pay for the foolish mistakes of her parents—even in the name of love. I had to be brave enough to give her my second greatest gift. The first gift was of life, the second was a chance for a balanced childhood with two parents.

I felt the burden of my decision had passed once and for all. The 96-hour limit had expired and I was no longer a mother. Now it would be far more difficult for me to change my mind. Yet, I was *still* a mother and I always would be. I felt terrible, but I felt better for having made my decision.

Exhausted, I finally fell asleep, knowing that my mother was probably lying awake in the other room, grieving the loss of her first and only grandchild.

And somewhere, in another corner of the city, a young couple was celebrating the adoption of a daughter, my daughter. I imagined them hugging each other in joy when the time limit had expired and their 'phone didn't ring. In their case, no news was good news.

I only hoped they knew the price we had paid.

11

Dearest Daughter

The get-away shopping spree had hurt more than it helped.

The following days hadn't been much better. But when my final decision was made and the clock ran out early Monday morning, I knew I had made the best decision for my daughter's sake. I was convinced that Keera's two adoptive parents could give her twice the time and love I could as a single parent.

On Monday evening, Mom came home from work and said, "Kayla, I know who the adoptive parents are."

My mouth dropped and I stared at her. "What?" Then when her words made sense to me, I asked, "How do you know?"

She told me a woman had come into the shop that day and knew I'd had a baby, so she asked how I was. Then she said she had some friends who had just adopted a baby—she wondered how that baby's birth mother was doing....

"I started asking questions," Mom said. "She described Keera perfectly—date and time of birth and everything. I put two and two
together. I told her, 'That's Kayla's baby; I know it is.' The poor woman
felt terrible." Mom's voice was quiet, her faint smile held a touch of
sadness.

"I know where they live—it's not far from the store."

I didn't know what to say.

Mom called the adoptive attorney and told him what she knew. He
told her the family was moving out of state. The adoptive father had a
new job in another state. There had been some delays in moving, but
they would be gone soon.

We didn't do anything with our knowledge, but it was a strange feeling to know exactly where my daughter was living.

That week, Mom and I went shopping for school clothes for me.
When we were in Younker's, I caught a glimpse of the children's department.

"Oh, Mom, look at the teddy bears," I said, tears filling my eyes. A
lump swelled in my throat; I thought I would break down right here in
the store.

"Do you want to buy one?" she asked.

I nodded. We searched, looking for the softest one we could find.
Anyone else would have said they all looked and felt alike. But I knew
different.

One was perfect for my daughter.

Later that day when we were home, Mom suggested I write a letter
to Keera explaining my feelings and actions. Someday, when she was an
adult, she could read it and know how I felt. I thought it was a good
idea.

I didn't know if my heart would ever stop aching for my baby. But I thought writing the letter might help. At least Keera would know how badly I wanted her. Now, as I sat at the kitchen table, I began to collect my thoughts. Next to me on the glass top sat the brown teddy bear wearing its plaid bow. Its unblinking eyes stared back at me.

Dearest Daughter,

I hope this letter will not be too painful for you to read. But believe me—it was extremely painful for me to write. By now you are probably a beautiful young lady and already know a couple of things about me. I just want you to know I will never forget you and how much I love you.

You were such a beautiful baby when you were born. I held you and fed you and spent as much time as I could with you during my three days in the hospital. You were such a good baby—you hardly cried at all—except when you were hungry. And I could tell you recognized my voice because you perked up when I spoke to you and you even smiled at me once or twice.

I want you to know how *hard* it was to let you go. I was 18 years of age and still living at home. Your father was in the Marines and we stopped seeing each other. Please understand I wanted only the best for you. I wanted you to grow up in a good home with both a mother and a father. I knew what it was like growing up without a father because my parents were divorced when I was six years old.

I picked out your adoptive parents from a list my lawyer, Bob Nash, had on file. I told him I wanted you to grow up in a Catholic environment with Catholic parents.

I did talk to your adoptive mother on the phone while I was in the hospital and I found out they were going to name you _____ Marie. I had named you Keera Michelle. I thought both were perfect names for such a pretty girl.

Your adoptive mother knew I was having a very rough time letting you go. She assured me you would someday find out about me, and know how desperately I wanted to keep you. She told me she had been adopted and she would know how you felt about this.

I stopped, got up and walked to my room for a tissue to blow my nose. I grabbed several, using one to wipe my eyes. I came back, picked up Teddy and hugged him, kissed his nose, then set him back down. He would go with the letter to the attorney, who would pass them along to the adoptive parents. I curled up and continued to write.

I will always treasure our three days together and all of the pictures I took of you. You will *always* have a special place in my heart and *I will never stop* loving you and wondering about you. It was the hardest decision I'm sure I will ever have made and I know I will have had doubts at first because of the absence I feel after carrying you for nine months and giving birth to you. But I know deep down inside, you will understand why I did what I did. It was not easy for me or my mother to let you go. We both cried for what seemed an eternity. My mother said you looked exactly like me when I was born. I can't help wondering if you will look like me when you get older.

If you ever want to try and find me or get a hold of me—I have left everything open so you can do so. It will have to be your decision, though. I would welcome you with open arms and never turn you away, believe me.

Always remember how much I love you and always will. You will always mean the world and more to me.

I will never forget you,

Love,
Your natural mother,
Kayla Becker

Mom read it over after I finished, suggested some minor changes and I wrote it again in my neatest penmanship. When I was done, she looked at it and said, "That's good, Kayla." She put her arm around me and gave me a hug.

That afternoon, I delivered my letter and the teddy bear to the attorney's office. I didn't have an appointment, but he said it was okay to see him then. He asked me how I was feeling. I said okay.

"I wrote this letter and bought a gift for the baby," I said. "I'd like to have you give it to the adoptive mother."

He said that was fine and he would take care of it. There was a silence while he waited for me to speak.

"I made my decision. I'm going to go through with it. It's for the best."

He nodded. "Then the adoptive parents can take the baby home now?"

"Yes, that's what I want for Keera."

I thought I should feel depressed when I left the office, but I didn't. I had been to the bottom of my own personal valley. It was time to begin climbing out.

The next day, I started school at Scott Community College. I half expected to wake up feeling sad and wanting to skip classes. But instead, I awoke in a good mood. I looked forward to establishing a routine; it would help me occupy my thoughts with other things. I felt better that the 96-hour waiting period was over. Writing the letter had helped me, too.

I had a good day at school. I felt positive about my new teachers and looked forward to completing the semester's work. The days fell into a schedule of classes and home life.

Mom and I talked about Keera on a daily basis. I was anxious for the pictures I took in the hospital to be developed. I had started a scrapbook filled with cards and notes—everything concerning Keera. It included Keera's birth certificate and all her legal papers. I treasured it, poring over it for hours, and sharing it with my friends with pride and love.

I knew they'd make a new birth certificate for my baby once the adoption had been finalized. That upset me at first. I didn't understand why they couldn't keep the same birth certificate. Mom said, "Well, Kayla, they just don't do that."

Jacqueline, Keera's adoptive mother, had agreed to contact me from time to time through the lawyer. I was so excited when she sent me a letter dated September 16, 1985:

Hello,

Your daughter is doing beautifully! She's strong and perfectly healthy.

My husband and I are so happy to finally have the opportunity of raising and loving a child. We thank you and we'll always remember the tremendous love and courage you showed.

The bear you gave is absolutely adorable. Thank you! It sits in her crib and she looks at it all the time. She'll have it forever and she'll know who gave it to her.

The letter you wrote to your daughter has been tucked away in a safe place until we feel she is prepared to read the contents. I think it's wonderful that you did that. I wish my mother had had enough foresight to write me a letter. I know your daughter will cherish it.

I'll be in touch. In the meantime, take care of yourself.

The adoptive mother

I was so grateful Jacqueline kept her word. I think she knew how hard it had been for me. I only wished the pictures would come from the hospital. The nurses promised I would get copies of the ones the hospital had taken.

It's normal procedure to take pictures of a newborn infant, but because Keera was an adoptive baby, they didn't do it right away. I was told they would have a professional photographer take them before Keera left the hospital, and I'd receive them in about a month.

Every day I went to the mailbox, searching for the photos. My heart was full of hope as I flipped through the letters, looking for anything that carried the hospital's return address. When there was nothing, I sighed my disappointment and went back in the house.

One day Mom said, "Kayla, something must be wrong. Why don't you call the hospital?"

So I called and a nurse told me, "Yes, they'll be coming soon."

The month of September passed and I still hadn't received them. I told Mom I couldn't imagine why it took so long. Mom insisted something was wrong. Finally, when I called the photography company, the receptionist checked and told me, "There's no record of Keera Becker pictures ever having been taken."

All I could manage to say was, "Mom, there are no nursery pictures."

"Kayla, there's got to be an answer for all of this," she said calmly.

Mom had learned to control her voice and body language in broadcast training. She seldom talked with her hands. But I knew with one look into her eyes that she was angry and troubled.

Mom dialed the hospital number and told the receptionist why she had called. She was put on hold before another nurse on the maternity floor responded. Mom explained the situation for a second time.

"There's got to be an explanation for these pictures. You assured us that they were taken."

A strange look came over my mother's face. It seems the pictures were taken the day before Mr. Nash left the hospital with Keera, but the photographer's camera malfunctioned for some reason and the photos didn't turn out.

This was too much for my mother. Her emotions had been tested severely over the past months.

"Oh, my God," Mom said. "What do you expect me to tell Kayla? Why wasn't she informed?" She started crying.

"My daughter has been going to the mailbox every day, looking for those pictures. Where are Kayla's rights in all of this? You people promised her nursery photos. What am I going to tell her? If she was a married mother, you would have told her!"

As I listened, I closed my eyes. I sat down and cried one more time since all of this had started.

Mom hung up the telephone and, without saying anything to me, called Carol Livermore, Jamie's Mom, for advice. Carol had been one of Mom's closest confidants during the pregnancy. Together, Mom and Carol decided the adoptive lawyer should be contacted.

I listened while Mom dialed the number and requested to speak with Bob Nash. When he answered, Mom's voice was filled with disappointment as she told him what she had learned. I knew that whatever comments he had used to pacify my distressed mother, it wasn't enough.

"Those pictures can't be taken again. She wants those pictures," she said. "She's so upset, Bob. Is there any chance she might be able to see the baby again before the family leaves town?"

At that, I stopped sobbing, and sat up straight.

"It's not going to hurt anything. Assure the adoptive parents that Kayla is no threat to them. She knows she made the right decision, but she wants to see that baby and she wants to be reassured.

"She has silly little fears," Mom continued. "She wants to hear it from the mother that the baby will someday hear how much Kayla loves her. She wants to hold that baby and see her again, because she knows the baby is moving out of state. I think it's very important."

She listened, nodding.

"We know who the parents are, we know where they live," she said, making her final point. "It's not your fault that I know, but I do. I can walk over there right now to see that baby if I choose to. But I won't do that to the adoptive mother. We're going through you.

"You see if you can arrange a meeting."

12

Meeting Keera's New Mother

I didn't have the nerve to go into the house.

I sat alone in the car, parked outside the social worker's home, talking to myself. "Maybe I should turn back," I said, hearing my voice tremble in the closed space. "I shouldn't have come; it will be too hard on me. Maybe it will be too hard on Jacqueline."

I already knew the adoptive father wouldn't be here—he'd thought it would too hard on him! And one of the conditions of my being here at all was that I had to come alone. Mom had agreed, but I knew she wanted to be here too.

Fear clutched at my heart as a cold sweat broke out on the small of my back. I was afraid to go in, but I couldn't leave. Inside this house was my baby, my daughter, and she was moving out of town soon. This was my last chance to see her for who knows how long? Maybe forever!

Someone slipped aside the drapery sheers and peeked out the window. I checked my face and hair in the rearview mirror. "You can't sit here forever, Kayla. They know you're here and they're waiting for you."

I took a deep breath, got out of the car and walked up to the door and knocked. A middle-aged woman wearing glasses answered the door of the tan and brown house. She introduced herself as Alice Johnson, the social worker who did the home study for the adoptive parents.

She smiled and I nervously responded.

"Jacqueline and the baby are in there," she said, indicating a doorway to the left. "I'll be in the other room if you need me, but I'll leave the three of you alone to get acquainted."

I walked in and a young, attractive woman sat next to my baby. Keera was on the floor on a white blanket.

My eyes filled with tears and I bit my lower lip. Keera looked so different! She was almost a month old and she had changed so much.

"Hi," Jacqueline said. She got up and hugged me. She had short, dark hair and wore gray slacks and a white sweater over a gray blouse with a large bow. She had long, dark eyelashes and a heart-shaped face. Her teeth were straight and white—definitely not the teeth of a cigarette smoker. I was glad Keera had a pretty mother.

"Hi," I said. I felt awkward and didn't know what else to say. My hands felt cold and clammy.

"Come over and see her." Jacqueline said.

I moved in for a closer look at my daughter. She seemed to be so alert, and she smiled. Keera was dressed in a little pink dress with pink pants, and her dark hair seemed thicker than I remembered it. I put my finger into her hand and she curled her little fingers around it. I was so close I could smell her baby sweetness.

"Remember me?" I asked. Keera gurgled her response.

We laughed. Keera had broken the ice between us. We were both here because we loved this baby girl. My tears continued to flow, but they were tears of joy. I was so grateful to see her again.

"Do you want to hold her?" Jacqueline asked. "It's about time for her bottle. You can give it to her."

She gently passed the baby to me. Her motions were smooth and confident. I remembered she had taught pre-school and wondered whether she'd ever worked in daycare with infants. Even if she hadn't, three weeks of taking care of Keera made her seem like an expert.

"She's so much bigger. I can't believe she's grown so much in such a short time!"

Jacqueline nodded, retrieved a prepared bottle from the kitchen and, when she had returned, handed it to me. "She's a good baby. She sleeps most of the night and she doesn't like to suck on a pacifier. If you let her suck your finger, she won't let go. Try it."

I did and laughed. I couldn't pull my finger out of her mouth, she sucked so hard.

For almost two hours, we talked with each other, held and loved Keera. We both knew she wasn't called Keera anymore, but we didn't discuss it.

Jacqueline told me about how she and the adoptive father met, and that she thought he was good-looking. She said he looked like TV's Magnum PI. She asked how my classes were going—she knew I was enrolled at Scott Community College—and wanted to know what I was majoring in. I told her business administration and she said her husband had studied that.

"Here, hold her head up higher so she doesn't choke while she eats," Jacqueline instructed.

As I held her, I listened, but my eyes and thoughts were on Keera. It felt like she wasn't my baby anymore. In the hospital, she had reacted to my voice, and touch. Now, as I watched Jacqueline with her, I could see Keera was reacting to Jacqueline. It hurt me to watch the two of them together, but I realized how good she was with the baby.

Jacqueline told me about her family, about Keera's already growing bank account, and their stable financial position. She gave me recently-taken pictures of my daughter.

"She'll never do without, Kayla," Jacqueline said.

I nodded. I was glad and at the same time jealous. This woman could do for my daughter all the things I couldn't.

The time flew by. I knew I should leave, but I didn't want to. When my stomach growled, I was reminded it was lunchtime and Jacqueline probably wanted me to leave. I began to say farewell.

I kissed my daughter and thanked Jacqueline for letting me see her again. Jacqueline hugged me again, and with tears streaming down my cheeks, I left. My arms ached with an emptiness that bit into my soul. It was the same feeling I'd had when leaving the hospital. But I knew I had done the right thing. Keera would be happy and she had good parents.

From the social worker's home, I drove straight to my mother's store. When I walked in, she came from behind the counter to greet me. Her eyes were full of questions, but she waited for me to speak.

I smiled at her and relief flooded her face as she smiled back. I knew how she must have worried.

"Mom, she's not my baby anymore," I said, fingering my purse. I hadn't had enough time to decide how I felt about that. Later, when I was alone, I would have time to look back over the visit.

Tears filled my mother's eyes as she looked at me. She didn't say anything, but waited for me to continue.

"I feel really good about the things we talked about. The adoptive mother is nice and she's pretty, too. She talked about how much work it is taking care of a baby."

Mom laughed. She knew. She'd raised three children mostly by herself.

"What else did she say?" Mom asked.

"She said she really appreciated what I had done for them. She promised over and over that they'd be good parents," I said, trying to remember all the things we'd talked about for two hours. "She promised she'd talk about me and wouldn't stand in the way if Keera ever wanted to come find me when she was older."

Everything seemed to have reached its conclusion. Although I still missed my daughter and wished I could have kept her, I felt good about my decision. As days passed, the grief lessened and a dull ache took over. Classes were going well and I had started to date again, this time a classmate. I told him on the first date that I had a daughter I'd released for adoption. His interest in me didn't seem to change and neither did the way he treated me.

He didn't pressure me into having sex and I was glad about that.

My life was manageable. I had been changed by my experience—I had grown up in a hurry and there were times when I felt older than students my same age.

I hadn't seen or heard from Stephen since early March. It was as if he had disappeared from the face of the earth. In late October, he wrote again.

He wanted to see me.

13

I Love You, Kayla!

When Stephen wrote to me, he begged for a picture of me and "your little girl." I hated it when he called Keera that. As if he hadn't had anything to do with her existence!

He said he hadn't dated anyone since a motorcycle accident he'd had. In early October, he'd been home on leave, and Jamie and I saw Stephen with some other guys at a football game. Jamie had dated one of them and wasn't getting along with him any longer. She practically hissed in my ear, "You better not talk to them or I won't speak to you for a week!"

It didn't matter. They avoided us like we had the plague. He explained why in his letter. One of the reasons was because he thought Jamie would give him a hard time. But telling me this wasn't his main reason for writing.

....I guess what I want to say is that I'd really appreciate a picture of you and maybe even a photo of your little girl. (If you can spare it, I'll understand if you can't.) I'll tell you what, Kayla, I would have actually asked you out when I was home, or the next time I am home....

He signed his letters, "Love, Stephen" and acted like everything that had happened was no big deal. As if carrying a child and giving birth to a daughter, then giving her up for adoption was unimportant compared to the "bar scene" or "new boyfriends" or the Iowa "Hawks." His letters fascinated me but at the same time, I was disgusted with him.

On the serious side of things, how are you doing concerning your little girl? I was wondering just what was going on in your head, reason being that I have really been kind of down about it. I guess I feel that I missed something in my life, or even both of our lives. I keep wondering what it would have been like if you, or even we, would have kept it. Am I just dumb, or did you feel like this at some time, Kayla? Was it my fault things are the way they are, could it have been different? God, Kayla, I wish I remembered your telephone number, I'd call right now. I have so many questions. I'm so confused. I'm sitting here alone at the Watch Desk at 2:00 in the morning, listening to Duran Duran and I start thinking about your girl.... sometimes I get so depressed. Am I going crazy? I feel like it at times.

Against my better judgment, I wrote back. I felt so sorry for him. How many times had he begged for forgiveness and sweet-talked me into going out with him? I had to admit I still felt something for him. After all, he was Keera's father.

Mom was really angry when I started dating Stephen again, but she couldn't talk me out of it. I only went out with him once or twice when he was home on leave. Even Jamie and my other friends were annoyed with me. Jamie, especially, couldn't understand how I could stand to look at him after the way he'd treated me.

We were out riding on his motorcyle one night, when he suggested we stop at his house for a soft drink. He knew I had pictures of Keera to show him. We sat shoulder to shoulder on the doghair-covered couch in his living room. I remembered the couple in the waiting room at the doctor's and how they'd acted. They'd been affectionate and loving. I wished we had that. And I wondered why Stephen waited until now to come back.

I wouldn't give him a photo to keep. They were much too precious; so I said I'd have copies made. But I never did.

I asked him if he thought Keera looked like me. And I wanted to see his baby pictures. He looked at one where she had her arm over her head—as if she were modeling—and said he used to do that a lot in his baby pictures.

He started crying. It surprised me and at the same time, I started too.

"I'm so sorry. I've been brainwashed and I can't believe I did this to you. I don't know what to say. I'm just so sorry."

After that, I saw Stephen a few times, but we didn't really date. He'd be gone and back home, but he wouldn't tell me when he was home. I'd be out with my friends and he'd come looking for me.

In October, Jacqueline wrote again and sent pictures. I lived for her letters! She'll never know how much they meant to me. I always made the time special when I read them. I stole away to my room and caressed each word over and over with my eyes. Later, I called all my friends and showed them the pictures and shared the letter. They all thought this baby was as beautiful as I did.

Dear Kayla,

These pictures were taken when she was 6 weeks old. She's really growing and developing. She's 23" long and weighs about 11 pounds. Her eyes are still a dark blue, but they're beginning to change. I see some brown creeping in. Her eyes are bright and incredibly alert. Her eyes will follow us for a short distance as we move around the room. She smiles *a lot* and coos. We play a little game with her where I'll coo and she'll coo back. It's so cute. We're carrying on conversation! She continues to sleep all night long (since she was 3 weeks!) and loves to suck on her fist or my pinky finger. She dislikes a pacifier.

It seems like a long time ago since we spoke. I certainly hope the meeting was helpful to you. I sincerely hope you're doing well.

Take care of yourself, Kayla. You'll hear from me again in about a month.

Jacqueline

Off and on, Stephen and I struggled with our relationship—mostly through our letters. I think I kept seeing what I thought were good qualities in him; I wanted to ignore the bad ones. I always thought he could change. I even thought he had.

But I was wrong.

I finally decided Stephen still wasn't ready to date just me. He always had another girl in line to take for a ride on his motorcycle. Usually, there were two. I knew I couldn't live with that—or him—for the rest of my life.

He kept pressuring me to resume the intimate relationship we had before he left for basic training. I didn't like it and I didn't want to take any chances. When he was away from home, he kept writing:

....You wonder what your life would be like if we wouldn't of ended up getting you pregnant? I wish I could answer that; I suppose things would be very different in your life and between us; but only you can answer that question. What would you like to have it been? No reason it can't be that way now. You are everything anybody could ever want, *you* have to make things happen in *your* life. What could possibly stop you from it, Kayla?....

One night he came up to me where I sat at a table with my friends.

"Kayla, I have to talk to you," he said. I looked at Eileen and Madge and went with Stephen to another table.

"I think we can make up for all the mistakes," he said. "I want to be married to you. I'm asking you to marry me. I've changed, I really have."

He took me by such surprise, that all I could say was, "What?" At first, I was really happy. But before I knew it, he was telling everyone that we were engaged!

I said, "Wait a minute. I don't see a ring on my finger. We're not engaged. You have to prove to me you've changed."

"What do I have to do to prove to you I've changed?" he asked. He didn't have the slightest idea.

"You figure that out," I said immediately.

He called me every day during the week. Then one night he was out and started making moves on a good friend of mine. She asked him, "How can you do that to Kayla?"

"Do what?" he asked.

When word reached me, I was disgusted with him. At that moment, I saw him as he really was. *Right*, I thought. *You've really changed.*

The next time he was home was around Thanksgiving 1986. When he came to find me, he walked up and said, "Hi." He started to say something else and I cut him off.

"Stay away from me. I don't ever want to see you again."

And I walked away.

The last letter I received from Stephen was postmarked November 12, 1986.

I wrote back a nasty response, giving him a piece of my mind. I didn't feel the least bit guilty for doing it.

He stuffed my letter back into an envelope with a sheet of typing paper. On it, he wrote a one-line response: "Cry me a river, Kayla. I was only trying to be nice."

Epilogue
Making Things Happen

A familiar car pulled up next to me at a stoplight. The driver waved, and sped away. He was half a block away before I realized who it was. "Oh, my gosh, it was Stephen!" I said, putting a hand to my face. My heart almost jumped out of my chest. I started shaking so bad, I had to pull over to the side of the road.

I haven't heard from him for almost a year now and I like it better that way. Jacqueline and I hadn't been in contact for some time now, either. That makes me sad, but I have no choice but to accept her decision.

She sent the last of her letters and pictures in early August, 1986. She wrote the attorney a letter; he passed on the photos with a letter of his own. He told me "she believes both they and you need to get on with your lives." He said he couldn't compel her to continue her letters, he felt we must accept her decision.

At first I was disappointed and sad, but I understood and at least knew what Jacqueline meant when she said we "need to get on with the rest of our lives." Still, I devoured her letter with my eyes, hungering for news of my daughter.

Kayla,

Hard to believe she's going to be a year old in a few short months. She is *very* active. You have to keep an eye on her at all times which can be exhausting!

Presently, she spends most of her waking hours standing and walking along furniture. She hasn't decided to stand by herself without assistance. I think by the end of the month she'll accomplish this feat. Soon after that, she'll be walking.

I don't know if you can tell by the pictures, but she has four teeth. The fourth one broke ground this month (an upper). Her first two appeared in her 8th month.

She's very affectionate and enjoys cuddling all her many stuffed animals. We have a cat she loves to rest her head on while she sucks her thumb. It's cute to see and the cat doesn't mind at all!

I laughed, imagining my little girl with her head nestled on the cat's belly. I could almost see her dark hair and pretty eyes looking up at me. It made a funny picture—one that made my heart long with yearning. She sounded so cuddly and adorable. Jacqueline's words made me so happy I wanted to dance, and at the same time so sad that hot tears came to my eyes. I knew she wasn't my little girl anymore. But I appreciated this small glimpse into her new life.

I continued to read Jacqueline's letter.

She used to take a morning and afternoon nap, but her morning nap is fading away as she's too busy exploring to take the time. Her afternoon nap she welcomes. (So do I!)

She loves books so several times during the day, I read to her. She also loves her rides in her stroller.

Another favorite of hers is swimming. I take her out to the pool and she'll jump off the side into my arms (from a sitting position). It's fun to see her delight at her accomplishments.

As for her eating habits, she hates carrots from the baby food jar, but if I cook them my way and mash them up, she'll eat them. Otherwise she enjoys all kinds of foods.

She's a lot of work and it's not all fun and games, but I really enjoy her. As with all children, she demands all my time and energy and then some. She's developing into quite a character and we share a lot of laughs.

She's strong, healthy and growing like a weed. She continues to have a happy and cheery disposition.. That about sums it up.

Take care, Kayla.

Sincerely,
Jacqueline

Shortly after I received the last batch of photos, I put them in my purse to show Jamie and Eileen. We were taking Eileen to a concert at the Col Ballroom, a large auditorium downtown, for her birthday. I drove and when we pulled into the parking lot, we decided not to take our purses inside. So we left them in the car after we had removed our money and driver's licenses.

After the concert was over, we returned to the car and discovered someone had broken in, stolen our purses and taken my photos with them. I was heartsick. They were the last photos of my daughter I might ever receive, and now they were gone. We reported the theft to the police, but nothing happened.

As of this writing, I'm getting ready to start my junior year in college, where I'll continue working toward a bachelor's degree. I have a boyfriend, but I'm dating with a new perspective on male and female relationships. I know there is no 100 percent way to prevent pregnancy and the price to pay for taking risks can be high.

I don't want to have another child until the circumstances are right.

I'm working parttime at the Handicapped Development Center in Davenport, and waiting tables in a restaurant near my mother's clothing store. I still see Heather quite often, and my other friends, Jamie, Madge, Eileen and Amy.

Whenever I see Heather, I can't help but look at Sara, her little girl. Heather had gone through much of the same experience I had, but she kept her baby and still lived at home until recently. Sara was born only a few weeks before Keera.

Every time I look at Sara, I imagine what Keera looks like now. She must be about the same size and close to the same stages in development. The pain has tapered off, but the memories are vivid. I still miss Keera and think of her constantly, even though she hasn't been called by that name for some time now. For me, she'll always be a tiny baby, my Keera, and I'll always remember her with the love a mother always has for her child.

When I think back on my pregnancy and all of the things that happened, I know there are reasons to be grateful. First of all, I'm glad I didn't choose abortion. No matter how much grief there is with having a baby and giving her up, I'm glad I gave my child the gift of life.

The second thing I'm grateful for is that my daughter was a healthy baby. My work at the Handicapped Development Center has made me realize how lucky I am to have had a strong, alert child who was given the chance for an active, full life.

The third thing that came out of this is the appreciation I have for my family and friends, who stuck by me and saw me through all of this. I gained new friends through the support services for pregnant teens and by meeting the adoptive mother. I'm grateful I have a mother and family who supported me. Not every teen has that.

I learned so much through this experience. I don't know if I'll ever trust anyone else as completely as I did Stephen—at least until I'm married. Now, I know better to ask questions and to be true to myself first. I won't be so accepting if a boyfriend ever says to me again, "It'll be all right."

The decision to release a baby for adoption is, I think, based on how strong you are. I don't think I'm all that strong, but I had a good support system of family and friends who gave me the facts and the space to make my decision.

To the young woman facing the same difficulties and challenges I did, I would say, "Consider adoption." I still think what I did was right. Although the emotional problems, agony and pain of my decisions seem insurmountable, I continue to feel comfortable and at peace in my own heart. The importance of the long-term welfare of my daughter was worth the pain.

Not long ago, a caring friend sent me a letter with a poem, "Child of My Heart," that she had written specifically for me. Jamie watched me as I read it:

Child of my heart, I remember the day
When I held you close in my arms.
The long months of waiting were over at last
And you had been born without harm.

Your tiny hand curled around my finger.
Oh, God! How could I let you go?

I wanted to clutch you back to my heart
The day your new mother came.
To take you to a home I could not share:
A new life, new family, new name.

Little girl, today you are one year old.
Oh, God! How did I let you go?

The words touched me and brought fresh, hot tears to my eyes. Birthdays are hard, but special in a way. That deep, deep ache that never goes away is always stronger on my daughter's birthday.

I light a candle for the child I lost
My tears put out the flame.
Yet a quiet joy grows in my heart
For the love I found when you came.

Help me, dear Father, to bear the pain.
Oh God! It was so hard to let you go!

The emotion swelling in my heart and body made me stop reading. This poet's words came from the heart. I could relate to them and they touched me deeply.

I gave you a life that makes sense of your birth:
A life with a future, a chance to grow.
Two parents to love you and guide your steps,
Two parents to teach you the things you should know.

Child of my heart, I'm your shadow birthmother
Thank God, I could let you go!

I will never stop loving my daughter. I love her today as much as I did during the first three days in the hospital—the only three days we had together. Sometimes I wish I had kept her and we could have continued our relationship forever. But I know I made the right decisions for her welfare.

There is peace in my life again.

Appendix A.

Teenage Pregnancy is Pandora's Box

In Greek mythology, there is a story of a woman, named Pandora, who had or found a jar—the so-called Pandora's box. According to the original version of the myth, it contained all kinds of misery and evil. When Pandora yielded to temptation and opened the jar, the evil flew out over the earth. Later versions told that *Hope* remained inside the jar.

So it seems to be with the issue of teenage pregnancy. Complex problems begin at conception and continue after the birth of the baby. The teen is faced with monumental decisions which will not only affect the future of the unborn child and her own future, but will painfully touch the lives of two entire families and all of the friends.

Elizabeth Stark, writing in *Psychology Today* magazine, notes that only 14 percent of teenage girls use contraceptives the first time they have intercourse. Frequently, it is months after sexual activity begins, that a young female visits a birth-control clinic. "And a major reason for a visit to a clinic is for a pregnancy test."

According to Dr. Wanda Franz, Vice President of the National Right to Life Committee, there are lifelong repercussions with the decisions made by the mother of an unplanned pregnancy or too-soon pregnancy. She maintains these repercussions don't have to be part of a completely negative experience.

"An unplanned pregnancy is not a good situation," says Dr. Franz. "No one wanted it to happen. Since it has, it's better to make the best of it and not allow yourself to be completely destroyed by the negative effects of it. What a young woman needs to do is take the crisis, and make it a potential for growth. She needs to take this time to look to the future, to set goals, and make plans for herself."

A pregnant teen in today's society has more decisions to make than her counterpart of 15-20 years ago. The old myth of the good girl/ bad girl no longer exists. In fact, many of the stories originally associated with an unwed pregnancy and adoption no longer hold true.

For example, it is no longer common for a pregnant teen to go into seclusion until the baby is born. In fact, guarding against isolation is strongly recommended by experts for emotional stability! Frequently, the young woman continues her education during her pregnancy. Society's attitude has changed toward the unmarried mother who keeps her baby. The unmarried mother today has several possible choices, and there are more support services available.

In 1973, the U.S. Supreme Court (Roe vs. Wade) legalized one of these choices: abortion. Since then estimates are that nearly 1.5 million abortions are performed each year. This fact, in addition to the accessibility of birth control measures, has decreased the number of infants available for adoption. The most influential societal trend, however, is the tendency for more unmarried teens to keep their infants, raising the child in a setting of single parenthood or with the assistance of an extended family setting.

A third choice is to release the newborn child for adoption. Traditionally, adoptions fulfilled the needs of two parties: birth parents who could not raise their infants and infertile couples who couldn't have their own children. According to William Pierce, Executive Director of the National Committee on Adoptions, there are two million couples who want to adopt. This averages out to 40 couples for every available baby.

For each of these important decisions—abortion, adoption or keeping the child—the future of the unborn child, and the health and well-being of the birthmother are at stake. The decision-making process determining the outcome of the pregnancy needs to be carefully worked through.

Joan Pincus is a social worker for Pregnancy Help, a pro-life emergency center in Brisbane, Australia. She works with women who have had abortions and/or have relinquished a child. Because abortion is considered a private, personal solution, she says grief may be internalized and expressed in other, often non-productive, ways.

In his book, *Spiritual Reflections of a Pro-Life Pilgrim*, Father Michael T. Mannion, S.T.L., M.A., Catholic Campus Minister and Director of the Newman Center at Glassboro State College, argues against abortion as the solution to an unplanned pregnancy.

"Abortion is a statement that violence is a 'legitimate and legal' means to solve social problems. In actuality, violence is equally disastrous in the womb or on the battlefield. The victims of both places point to humankind's inability to be at peace with itself, and both situations have their roots in the same failure of people to see and take seriously their own dignity and worth.

"The woman herself is the second victim in an abortion [the unborn child being the first] and the destruction of one life will never bring healing to another. No human life is a mistake, even though the manner of the conception may be less than favorable and even sinful.

"We [need to] refuse to invalidate and destroy the gift simply because the timing is inconvenient and the circumstances awkward.... The child's only sin is that he or she comes at the wrong time and the wrong place: an inconvenience—to a college schedule, an employment situation or a lifestyle plan."

Father Mannion continues, "....The guilt and loneliness felt by a woman who has had an abortion is more often than not accompanied by a sense of worthlessness, inadequacy and inability to help others, let alone herself...."

Only three percent of the one million plus abortions in the United States each year involve the "hard cases" (i.e., rape, incest, physical complications, handicaps). Father Mannion says there is mounting evidence indicating that even in these cases, abortion has not been a solution, but only a cause for further anguish.

Vicky Thorn, coordinator of Project Rachel and co-director of the Respect Life Office of the Archdiocese in Milwaukee, Wis., says a woman who has had an abortion may spend anywhere from five to ten years in a state of denial before showing symptoms of post-abortion syndrome, or aftermath. The smallest symbols related to the abortion—a cookie eaten immediately following the procedure, the suction of a vacuum cleaner, the sight of a pregnant woman or couples with children—may send her into a state of anxiety and dysfunction.

Several recent studies have shown that young women who choose abortion as a means to solve the problems of pregnancy may have lifelong emotional turmoil. Says Mary Beth Seader, MSW, the National Committee on Adoption, "Once you're pregnant, you're a mother to that child forever." Experts say many young women become pregnant

again very quickly, subconsciously trying to replace the aborted baby—
even to the extent that every time the baby moves within her, she thinks
not of this baby, but the one she has aborted.

"Almost anything can send her into a reliving of the abortion experience," says Thorn. "She may fixate on a child near the same age as her
child would have been, the date the abortion occurred or the due date
which would have been her child's birthday. She may be involved in al-
cohol or drug abuse, sexual promiscuity or sexual dysfunction—none of
which she relates to the abortion. But in hindsight, we know all of these
symptoms are related."

This "interruption" in a young person's life plan can be developed
into something positive, however, provided the decisions are ones the
teen mother can live with in peace.

Says Dr. Wanda Franz: "For a lot of young girls, there is a sudden
realization that maturity means taking responsibility for their actions,
and doing the right thing.... giving the baby up for adoption is a loving,
caring response to the child. Having 'made a mistake,' it's important to
realize it was not the child's mistake and this baby needs the best possible chance in life."

The alternative to adoption is keeping the child. A study conducted
by a non-profit organization dedicated to preventing unwanted teenage
pregnancies, the Center for Population Options, has revealed that teen
pregnancies cost the nation $16 billion annually. Of the 385,000 first-
born babies of adolescents in 1985, $6 billion in welfare benefits will be
paid to the mothers over the next 20 years.

Welfare and other governmental costs through programs like Aid to
Families with Dependent Children, Medicaid and food stamps as well
as administrative costs for these programs cost $16.6 billion in 1985.

"For a few of these girls," says Helen Brown, a counselor to pregnant teens in Davenport, Iowa, "this is a way of life. Each new child means a larger welfare check. It's like getting a raise in allowance. The bulk of our students, however, come from homes where more traditional values are accepted. The pregnancy is a real trauma in their lives."

For many young women who keep their babies, the standard of living and level of education are less than that of their peers. According to Frank L. Mott and William Marsiglio, writing in *Family Planning Perspectives:* "Teenagers who give birth while in high school . . . are far less likely to graduate from high school (with a regular diploma or equivalent certificate) than are women who delay child bearing until their 20s."

According to literature written on the subject, one of ten teenage girls in the United States becomes pregnant every year and almost half of these pregnancies result in births—30,000 of them to girls under the age of 15.

Teens are becoming sexually active at a younger age. And instead of protecting themselves from pregnancy, they assume "it won't happen to me." Counselor Helen Brown calls it the "head-in-the-sand-syndrome." To plan for sex, teens say, is a bigger sin than responding to the circumstances of the moment. Says Linda Cloghessey, a childbirth educator, "girls today don't want to use birth control because it marks them with their peers as 'easy.' It's all right if intercourse takes place because it's spontaneous or unplanned. So they take their risks and hope they won't get caught."

Once they are "caught," all experts stress the value of having supportive parents. Says Kathryn Bohn, Kayla's mother: "Parents, no matter how disappointed or angry they are, need to recognize it's important to support the teenager. You've got to help your daughter deal with this. You've got to help her hold her head up. Don't let this nine months of her life ruin your relationship. It's not worth it. Teenage pregnancy is one of the worst fears of parents, but when it happens, it doesn't have to be the end of the world. Your daughter feels bad enough without the added pressures of condemning and verbally abusive parents."

Betty, Janet, Lisa, Meredith, Elizabeth and Melanie (names are changed as a matter of T.A.P.P. policy), all of whom have experienced a teenage pregnancy, offer this advice to parents:

* Get a head start on the misinformation about conception which is passed among students in grade school, junior high and high school. Educate your child early on in his or her life.

* Talk more, don't be afraid to communicate with your daughter or son about sexual activity. Long before the age of 12-14, parents should discuss sex with their teenagers.

* Don't assume that because a young woman uses birth control pills she will be more sexually active.

* If your daughter is pregnant, don't reject her or condemn her for being "a bad girl."

The young women in this story—Kayla, Jamie, Eileen, Madge, Amy and Heather, in addition to six teen mothers (Betty, Janet, Lisa, Meredith, Elizabeth and Melanie)—have other words of advice for their peers. They say the heartaches of an unplanned pregnancy change life but do not necessarily ruin it. Although it may sound simplistic, they recommend not becoming sexually active before you're ready to accept responsibility for your actions. "But if you're going to be sexually active, protect yourself," says Elizabeth. "Don't rely on your partner to look out for you. You've got to abstain or protect yourself."

Dr. Franz says that teenage pregnancy will continue to be a problem as long as children, and adults who are behaving like children, refuse to take responsibility for their behavior. What needs to be taken into account is that "when you engage in sexual behavior, even if you use some sort of contraception, you are setting yourself up to reproduce. There is no 100 percent successful way to avoid getting pregnant if you're sexually active."

Says Kayla, "Everyone thinks it won't happen to her. A relationship can move too fast and you don't know what you're getting into until it's too late. I've learned it's important to think more about watching out for yourself.

"The risks are too great," she continues. "You don't know what pain and turmoil you could cause for yourself and others until it happens to you. And then it's too late."

Once a teenager suspects she is pregnant, experts recommend a plan of action.

1. Don't panic. Slow down! Don't make any decisions in a crisis mode. Don't make any decisions by yourself. You have time to analyze your options. Any decisions you make will be a part of your life; *informed* decisions will benefit all concerned.

2. Talk with someone who can help you think clearly about your choices. This could be a pastor, parent, or a trained expert in emergency pregnancy counseling. If you're afraid to tell your parents, a trusted counselor or support person may be able to help.

3. If you feel as though abortion is your only choice, you need to talk with someone who can help you study the risks involved. Sterility, infertility, or post-abortion syndrome can result. You will have to live with your decision for a lifetime.

Ask yourself these questions: Why do you feel the need for an abortion? Because of your boyfriend? family? friends? money? How will this answer solve your problem? If you're looking at what appears to be a "monumental wall," consider examining the "wall" by its pieces.

4. Once you decide to carry the baby to delivery, medical care is of the utmost importance for you and the health of your child. If you don't know of local or regional agencies, the national ones listed in Appendix B will be able to help. If you are unable to pay for services, there is assistance available.

5. At some point, you must tell your parents, and ask for their support. It may be helpful to start a plan of medical care as a visible means of responsibility on your part toward coping with the problem.

You will want someone to go through the birthing process with you. This could be your mother, a trained professional (birth educator), or a "big sister" who has offered to help you. Although it's less common, the father of your child may want to be there. This same person may offer support if you decide to release your baby for adoption.

6. If housing becomes a problem, emergency support counselors will help you find a place to live. There are foster home shelters, small group homes, or larger facilities available. Legal services, if necessary, are also available at low or no cost to those in need.

7. You will need to decide whether you plan to keep the baby or release him or her for adoption. If you plan to keep the baby, there are emergency pregnancy services which will help provide support and baby necessities.

8. If you decide to release your baby for adoption, your counselor will help make a referral to a state-licensed agency. If you opt for a private adoption through a friend, relative, attorney, or physician, you will need to make these arrangements.

9. Despite all pressure from family, friends, or anyone else, decide now that you will make your own decisions. Acknowledge that this will be a painful time in your life and you most likely will need to grieve no matter what your decision. Seek expert counseling and information. Base your decisions on a body of information and informed consent, rather than hurriedly-made, pressure-based outside opinions.

* * *

Most teens don't know what to do until they've sought counseling. Experts agree it's important for the mother to feel she has some options.

"A lot of girls don't make up their minds about keeping the baby or adoption until after they've delivered," says Dr. Franz. "That probably should be left open as an option for the mother. She can always decide, she doesn't have to feel locked into a decision early on in the pregnancy. Each mother needs to be ready to make this decision. The medical and psychological needs can be worked through, often with the financial help of the parents, various organizations, or an adoptive couple."

Once a young mother decides she's not going to abort the baby, then she must make the decision of keeping the baby or giving him or her up for adoption. Adoption needs to be presented in a caring, life-giving way, says Thorn.

Perhaps a look at some successful adoptees would be helpful. Former President Jerry Ford; the Olympic Gold Medal ice skaters, the Carruthers twins; James "Dano" McArthur on TV's Hawaii Five-O program and son of actress Mary Martin's son—these are all successful adoptees. Comedian Bob Hope and his wife, Delores, adopted four children!

Making this decision, however, is difficult, says Dr. Franz. Teenagers are more inclined to think in terms of concrete effects. For example, a teenager realizes the baby is lovable and touchable. He or she is a reality. To give a baby up for adoption makes everything seem more like an abstract notion. It takes him or her out of reality.

"Teenagers have difficulty thinking through what it would be like for their child to live with someone else, and to imagine the circumstances as positive," she says. "It helps to 'paint a picture' in concrete terms of what the alternatives are—and what their baby's life will be like if they keep him or her. It's also a good idea to look at families who have adopted and what it has meant in their lives to raise a child."

There are many ways to legally release a baby for adoption. *Traditional adoptions* are handled through a licensed agency by trained, professional counselors who are capable of counseling all parties of the adoption triangle. Adoptions frequently are being handled by attorneys, physicians and some non-state agencies.

Open Adoption allows the birthmother to meet the adoptive parents, exchange information, and share in the life of the child within restrictions. *Semi-open adoption* may provide for initial meetings and some sharing of photographs and information about the life of the child.

Regardless of the path selected, the birthmother has some freedom to express her preferences for an adoptive family. Says Vicky Thorn, coordinator of Project Rachel, "It's important in the issue of open or semi-open adoption, that the birthmother realizes the baby will always be her child, but not for daily contact. She is relinquishing rights so that the baby can become part of a permanent family."

Planning the child's future is an important decision. Social workers Janice Beerman and Alice Stephens, writing in *Heartbeat* magazine, suggest that the mother make an honest evaluation of her situation to help with the decision. They recommend the following considerations:

1. Make a list of the pros and cons of keeping the child and of placing the child for adoption.

2. Imagine what your life will be like in one year, five years, 10 years from now without the child.

3. List your future plans and goals and describe how the child will fit into these goals.

4. Describe the ideal situation for having a child—what's the appropriate timing, partner, financial situation, living situation, job, etc.? How does your actual situation compare to your expectations?

5. Describe your good parenting skills. What attributes, personality traits, do you believe parents should possess? How do you fit the picture?

6. What decisions have you made in the past and how did you come to those decisions?

7. List some of the problems someone might face if she kept her baby or placed her baby for adoption? Which problems do you think you have? Which set of problems do you think you could best handle and live with?

8. How have your parents, friends, and the natural father reacted to the pregnancy? What do they think you should do and how important are their opinions to you? What would happen if you didn't take their advice? Are you independent enough to make this decision without being influenced by these people?

9. Describe a child's physical and emotional needs and how you would fulfill those needs.

10. How much time, energy and effort on your part do you think a child requires and demands?

11. If you are thinking in terms of keeping the baby, develop a plan which shows where you will live, how you will support the baby, how you will continue your educational plans, and how you will assume your parental responsibilities, social life and job?

12. If you keep the baby, make a list of those who have offered to help you and the kinds of help they have offered. Describe your back-up plan if those offers fall through.

13. If you were to place the baby for adoption, how will you handle the comments, questions, and criticisms that you face from others? How do you anticipate handling your own feelings of loss, sadness, grief or regrets that you may experience?

14. Have you ever known anyone who was adopted? How do they feel about being adopted? How do they feel about their birthmothers?

15. Talk to an adoptive parent and to someone who has placed a child about their experiences and feelings.

* * *

All experts agree that a young woman will experience grief for the loss of her child, whether she aborts or releases the baby for adoption. It is the experience of losing a loved one.

According to social worker Joan Pincus, the memories will remain, but the pain itself will ease. "Thus if the grief is allowed to run its 'normal' course, it is a healing process—painful at first, but gradually tapering off."

A survey of unmarried women by Donald Gough in 1971 revealed facts that are still relevant today. In his work, "Adoption and the Unmarried Mother," he learned:

1. Girls have considerable guilt and depression about the situation;

2. Although firmly decided on adoption, there is always a part of her that wants to keep the baby;

3. There are great emotional difficulties about parting from the baby; and

4. When they do part from the baby, they need help in mourning their loss.

More and more young women who release their babies for adoption are taking positive steps to mourn the loss and reach a stage called "closure." Kayla did these things—holding her baby, keeping photos, preparing a scrapbook, writing a letter, buying the baby a gift, and meeting the adoptive mother—but she didn't know they were recommended by experts. She did what was demanded by her love, grief and mourning. Even though parting may be made more difficult, the end result is that the young mother who performs these acts may be able to live in more peace with the decision she has made.

Regardless of whether a young woman choosing adoption decides to follow any or all of these recommendations, Pincus says these changes in attitude toward the relinquishing mother are helping her resolve her grief.

Pincus writes that "people need to know what it is that they are mourning."

"Thus, for some girls who place their babies for adoption, grieving can be less painful if the girl has actually seen her baby, and knows what she is mourning."

It is helpful to be able to say that she has done everything within her capabilities to give her child a healthy, happy life—and to make the best possible decision for the baby, and herself.

It is important for the young woman to make definite plans for her own future. Says Vicky Thorn: "It's important to encourage her to continue her education. If she keeps the baby, education is the only thing that's going to break the cycle of poverty."

Although this is one of the challenges faced by teenagers in general, Dr. Franz says that "if you're in crisis, and an unplanned pregnancy is definitely a crisis, that's usually a time when you can take advantage of it and mature.

"A very important component of growing up is being goal-oriented, planning ahead and working toward goals," she says. "I don't see how you can make a choice about keeping the baby without looking at the future and starting to deal with it in a very real way. I think that's a goal for anybody, whether they're experiencing an unplanned pregnancy or not. During a crisis is a logical time to plan for the future."

Once a teenager is pregnant, there are no easy answers, says Mary Beth Seader, a social worker with the National Committee on Adoption.

"But there *are* answers. I've seen some teens come through a pregnancy and it's the best thing that ever happened to them," says Seader. "They found help, and put their lives back on the right track. It was an opportunity for growth."

Every pregnant teenager and others concerned with her who have peered inside Pandora's Box have the opportunity to make the most of its contents. How will you respond? Will you allow eternal Hope to escape in the form of life . . . for a healthy and happy future for yourself and your child?

Says Kayla: "To the young woman facing the same difficulties and challenges I faced, I would say, 'Consider adoption.' I still think what I did was right. Although the emotional problems, agony and pain of my decisions seemed insurmountable, I continue to feel comfortable and at peace in my own heart. The importance of the long-term welfare of my daughter was worth the pain."

Appendix B.
Where to Go For Help

The following national organizations are committed to serving young women experiencing an unplanned pregnancy, those suffering from the results of an abortion or an adoption, or providing education and information. They are grouped in four main categories, although services provided by some programs may overlap somewhat: Crisis Pregnancy Counseling; Post Abortion Counseling and Healing Services; Pregnancy Support and Adoption Services; and Education and Information Organizations. Many national programs offer *Hotline* or "Toll Free" 800 numbers.

To find help, experts suggest starting with your local pastor or priest. Or look in the telephone book for a church-related social service agency or an inter-faith one which will answer your questions, offer support, and help guide you through a decision-making process.

For local social service agencies serving the needs of pregnant teenagers, consult the business pages of your telephone directory for local offices of the national programs (i.e., Birthright, Inc. may have an office in your area), or the yellow pages under such headings as Birth

Control Information Centers, Birth & Pregnancy Assistance, Family and Children's Services, Pregnancy Counseling, and Social Service Organizations.

Once you have taken this initial step, many agencies will either provide for your needs, or will make referrals for specific services, such as medical care, maternity clothing, foster home or residency shelters, and birth-related or general educational programs.

CRISIS PREGNANCY COUNSELING

Bethany Christian Services
901 Eastern Ave.
Grand Rapids, MI 49503
(616) 459-6273

Bethany Christian Services
475 High Mountain Rd.
North Haledon, N.J. 07508
(201) 427-2566

Birthright, Inc.
686 North Broad St.
Woodbury, N.J. 08096
(609) 848-1818
NATIONAL HOTLINE: 1-800-848-LOVE
CANADA HOTLINE: 1-800-328-LOVE

Catholic Charities U.S.A.
1319 F St. NW
Washington, D.C. 20004
(202) 639-8400

Child Welfare League of America
67 Irving Place
New York, N.Y. 10003
(212) 254-7410

Child Welfare League of America absorbed the Florence Crittendon Association. These homes provide maternity services and placement of infants.

Holy Family Services Counseling & Adoption
357 S. Westlake Ave.
Los Angeles, CA 90057
(213) 484-1441

Lifeline of Southwest Pennsylvania
Dept. L
713 Investment Bldg.
Pittsburg, PA 15222
(412) 562-0700

Hotlines:

Butler Office: (412) 282-1200
Beaver Office: (412) 843-0505
728-5621
Cranberry Township: (412) 776-2550
Mon Valley: (412) 489-9020
Downtown Pittsburg: (412) 562-0543
Connellsville: (412) 628-5555

An emergency pregnancy service. Counseling, 24-hour hotline, pre-pregnancy testing, professional referrals, confidentiality, assistance with maternity and childcare needs, personal support, volunteer sessions, educational programs, speakers bureau, and CARE (counseling abortion related experiences).

Salvation Army
799 Bloomfield Ave.
Verona, N.J. 07044
(201) 239-0606

Provides emergency housing to pregnant teens on occasion.

Save-a-Baby
Box 2700
Lynchburg, VA 24506
1-800-847-6810

Y.W.C.A. of the U.S.
726 Broadway
New York, N.Y. 10003
(212) 614-2700

Women's Health Services

Kenmore Mercy Hospital
2950 Elmwood Ave.
Kenmore, N.Y. 14217

St. Jerome Hospital
16 Bank St.
Bativia, N.Y. 14020

Hotlines:

(716) 879-6280

(716) 343-6047

Free pregnancy testing and professional counseling. Prenatal care, residential care, if needed. Delivery follow-up with responsible adolescent care training and adoption and foster care services.

POST ABORTION COUNSELING AND HEALING SERVICES

Alternatives to Abortion International
World Federation of Prolife Emergency Pregnancy Service Centers
8 Cottage Place
White Plains, N.Y. 10601
(914) 683-0901

There are approximately 1,700 Prolife Emergency Service Centers in the United States and abroad. Referrals are provided to local agencies. Services include non-discriminatory, non-judgmental support for the woman distressed by pregnancy. Services include free pregnancy testing, counseling, referrals to private home shelters, financial and medical guidance, maternity clothes and baby needs, and referrals to existing agencies where needed and when requested.

American Victims of Abortion
419 Seventh St. NW, Suite 402
Washington, D.C. 20004

Open Arms (Abortion Related Ministries)

Sue Thurber	or	Debra Kerr
P.O. Box 667		9015 E. 135th Pl. S.
Glenpool, OK 74033		Bixby, OK 74008
(918) 321-9128		(918) 369-3837

Ministers to all those who are experiencing an unplanned pregnancy or are suffering as a result of an abortion: mothers, fathers, grandparents, friends, relatives, medical professionals and counselors. Open ARMS and additional pro-life literature is distributed and speakers are provided upon request.

Project Rachel
Office of Respect Life
Archdiocese of Milwaukee
3501 S. Lake Dr.
Milwaukee, WI 53201
(414) 769-3450

Women Exploited
1068 Bland St.
Norfolk, VA 23513
(804) 855-7443

Women Exploited by Abortion (WEBA)
P.O. Box 11720
Kansas City, MO 64138
(816) 537-6668

Support system for women who have had abortions. Chapters are located in many states.

PREGNANCY SUPPORT AND ADOPTION SERVICES

Adoption Service Information Agency
7720 Alaska Ave. N.W.
Washington, D.C. 20012
(202) 726-7193

Edna Gladney Home
2300 Hemphill
Fort Worth, TX 76110
1-800-433-2922

Evangelical Adoption & Family Service
201 S. Main St.
Room 200
North Syracuse, N.Y. 13212
(315) 458-1415

Evangelical Child & Family Agency
1530 N. Main St.
Wheaton, IL 60187
(312) 653-6400

Golden Cradle Home
555 E. City Ave.
Bala Cynwyd, PA 19004
(215) 668-2136

Maternity & Adoption Services
1514 Peniston St.
New Orleans, LA 70115
(504) 895-0646

The National Committee for Adoption
1346 Connecticut Avenue NW
Suite 326
Washington, D.C. 20036
(202) 463-7559
Hotline: (202) 463-7563

Plan Loving Adoptions Now
203 East 3rd St.
P.O. Box 667
McMinnville, OR 97128
(503) 472-8452

Smithlawn Maternity Home & Adoption Agency
702-76th St.
P.O. Box 6451
Lubbock, TX 79493
(806) 745-2574

St. Francis Home
P.O. Box 6068
Hoboken, N.J. 07030
(201) 798-9059

Provides child care, educational referrals, job search counseling, public assistance, shelter and support to women keeping their babies.

EDUCATIONAL AND INFORMATIONAL ORGANIZATIONS

Baptists for Life
P.O. Box 3158
Grand Rapids, MI 49501
(616) 459-9809

The Christian Action Counsel
701 Broad St.
Falls Church, VA 22046
(703) 237-2100

Lutherans for Life
275 North Syndicate
St. Paul, MN 55104
(612) 645-5444

An interfaith Lutheran organization working to strengthen the existing common bond of concern for life among Lutherans, and to develop and distribute educational materials and respond to the needs of people including families, children, unwed mothers, the handicapped, elderly and unborn.

National Committee for a Human Life Amendment
1430 K St. NW, Suite 800
Washington, D.C. 20005
(202) 393-0703

National Organization of Episcopalians for Life
10523 Main St.
Fairfax, VA 22030
(703) 591-NOEL

About 70 local chapters addressing local needs. National group disseminates pro-life material, prepares a bi-monthly newsletter and urges members to be aware of legislation for support of pro-life issues.

National Right to Life Committee
419 7th St. NW, Suite 402
Washington, D.C. 20004
(202) 626-8800

National Youth Pro-life Coalition
Hastings-on-Hudson
New York, N.Y. 10706
(914) 478-0103

Office of Pro-life Activities
National Conference of Catholic Bishops
1312 Massachusetts Ave., NW
Washington, D.C. 20005
(202) 659-6673

Pearson Foundation, Inc.
3663 Lindell Blvd., Suite 290
St. Louis, MO 63108
(314) 652-5300

Provides research materials to pro-life centers. Includes audio-visuals, a manual and pamphlets as well as other printed materials. Success rate is 80 percent of abortion-bound women.

Presbyterians Pro-life
Research, Education and Care, Inc.
P.O. Box 2153
Decatur, GA 30031
(612) 861-5346

Southern Baptists for Life
Box 470050
Tulsa, OK 74147
(918) 749-5022

Appendix C.

Recomended Reading*

Arms, Suzanne. *To Love and Let Go*. (New York: Knopf, 1983). Photographs feature birth and adoptive parents, and adoptees.

Burgess, Linda Cannon. *The Art of Adoption*. (New York: W.W. Norton & Company, 1981).

Kuenning, Delores A. *Helping People Through Grief*. (MN.: Bethany House, 1987). Comfort for victims of abortion or for those suffering from adoption, in addition to many other life experiences.

Lindsay, Jeanne Warren. *Pregnant Too Soon: Adoption is an Option*. (St. Paul, Minn.: EMC Publishing, 1981).

Mannion, Michael T. *Abortion & Healing: A Cry to be Whole*. (Kansas City, MO: Sheed and Ward, 1986).

Mannion, Michael T. *Spiritual Reflections of a Pro-Life Pilgrim*. (Kansas City, MO: Sheed and Ward, 1987).

Sorosky, Arthur D., M.D.; Baran, Annette, M.S.W.; and Pannor, Reuben, M.S.W. *The Adoption Triangle*. (New York: Anchor Press/Doubleday, 1978).

*Books are listed with teens in mind.